START DAY TRADING NOW

Anyone Can Day Trade!

Includes:

Entry & Exit Strategies

Daily Trading Checklists

Startup Costs & Considerations

Risks & Benefits | Market Indicators

MICHAEL SINCERE

Author of the bestselling *Understanding Options* and *All About Market Indicators*

adamsmedia

AVON, MASSACHUSETTS

Published by Adams Media, a division of F+W Media, Inc.
57 Littlefield Street, Avon, MA 02322. U.S.A.
www.adamsmedia.com

ISBN 10: 1-4405-1186-1
ISBN 13: 978-1-4405-1186-8
eISBN 10: 1-4405-1192-6
eISBN 13: 978-1-4405-1192-9

Printed in the United States of America.

10 9 8 7 6 5 4 3

Library of Congress Cataloging-in-Publication Data
is available from the publisher.

This publication is designed to provide accurate and authoritative information with regard to the subject matter covered. It is sold with the understanding that the publisher is not engaged in rendering legal, accounting, or other professional advice. If legal advice or other expert assistance is required, the services of a competent professional person should be sought.
—From a *Declaration of Principles* jointly adopted by a Committee of the American Bar Association and a Committee of Publishers and Associations

Many of the designations used by manufacturers and sellers to distinguish their product are claimed as trademarks. Where those designations appear in this book and Adams Media was aware of a trademark claim, the designations have been printed with initial capital letters.

This book is available at quantity discounts for bulk purchases.
For information, please call 1-800-289-0963.

DEDICATION

To my mother and father,
who never stopped believing in me,
or in what I could achieve.

PRAISE FOR *START DAY TRADING NOW*

Sincere tackles a very difficult task: teaching someone—who knows nothing about trading—how to day trade. He does a good job of explaining the various tools (indicators, charts, etc.) that can provide guidance and clues for making the "buy" decision. Sincere shows the reader how to protect assets with stop-loss orders and issues plenty of warnings about the complexity of the job. The reader should grasp the necessity of beginning gently and having the patience to gain useful experience before entering into the fray with real money.

—Mark D. Wolfinger, author *The Rookie's Guide to Options*

Contents

CHAPTER 8

Doing Your Homework • 173

PART 1
GETTING STARTED

Before we begin, I want to thank you for taking the time to read my book.

I'm delighted you're willing to make the effort to learn more about day trading, a fascinating but often misunderstood way to make money. Be prepared to learn a lot of information in a short time period. I've included explanations and definitions of terms that may be unfamiliar to you in the book itself. These words, italicized in the text, are also included in a glossary at the back to help you keep informed.

In this part, I'll show you how to set up an account and a home office, and how to use specialized tools to make your first trade. That's the easy part. The hard part is using all of that information to increase earnings. Although you're about to take an educational and entertaining journey, my ultimate goal is to teach you to become a better trader while helping you to manage risk.

And now, let's get started.

The Opening Bell: What Is Day Trading?

Day trading, or intraday trading, is a method that works just like it sounds: you enter a trade involving one or more stocks (or another security) and exit the trade—which you've only held onto for seconds, minutes, or hours—by the end of the day. It's only semantics, but in this book I often refer to day trading as a strategy. You could also call it a technique, style, or activity. The goal is to make a trade and exit with a profit—the sooner the better—and still get a good night's sleep.

Note to overseas readers: While the content of this book was written with the U.S. stock market in mind, the information included in this book can be applied to any stock market you trade on.

Myths Versus Reality

Many myths about day trading exist. Because uninformed traders have made mistakes in the past, many people think that day trading is too risky. They incorrectly believe that day traders are chained in front of a computer ten hours per day, making hundreds of lightning-fast trades while scooping up $500 worth of pennies.

Although a handful of individuals may fit this stereotype, many modern day traders are choosier about the trades they make. They tend to trade smarter and make only a handful of transactions a day. Rather than being highly active traders (making hundreds of trades a day), some day traders prefer being high-probability traders (trading when the odds are in their favor). It's really a personal choice what kind of trader you will be.

Day trading doesn't mean you'll be able to lounge in front of a pool in Europe while trading on a laptop or cell phone. Although some lackadaisical traders have made transactions while on never-ending vacations, it's unlikely they'll be profitable for long when trading in this environment. Why not? Most day traders need to focus like a laser beam on their screen without distractions; they have to be alert and at the top of their game at all times.

Traders work very hard—they may put in fifty- to sixty-hour workweeks. Plus, they're responsible for their own taxes, tech support, and education. They have to make lightning-fast decisions, and if they're wrong, it could cost them money. Without a regular paycheck, many traders feel tremendous pressure to overtrade to make money. Because the markets are always changing, traders must also constantly evolve and adapt to market conditions. A strategy that works well one year may not work the following year.

Even with all of these challenges, it is possible to be a successful day trader, but you'll have to work hard at it.

On the plus side, it also means being in control of your time and your schedule. You don't have to commute to an office and report to a boss. It's extremely satisfying to find a good trade and be rewarded for it in money. And don't forget that you can trade from anywhere in the world, there's no dress code, and you have the freedom to set your own financial goals.

Some traders have combined the best of both worlds by trading part-time. For example, you could initiate a trade in the morning and set up automatic triggers to sell when the stock hits a certain price. In this case, day trading is simply another strategy that is used when market conditions are right. You'll learn about the benefits of part-time trading in the next chapter.

Why Read This Book?

If you're a rookie trader and want to learn more about day trading, you've come to the right place. You'll learn how to incorporate day trading strategies into your trading portfolio. And if you're thinking of becoming a full-time day trader, by the time you finish this book, you will have a better idea if day trading is for you. No matter what kind of trader you are, many of the lessons you'll learn in this book will be invaluable. I will also help you avoid some of the most common trading pitfalls.

If you're reading this book out of curiosity or entertainment, I'll try my best to meet your needs. Like all my other books, I try to explain day trading as if you were sitting across from me at my kitchen table. My goal is to save you time and money while educating and engaging you.

You'll learn:

- How to get started, including how much money you'll need, how to choose and use a broker, and how to set up a trading account.
- How to read charts—an essential tool for day traders.
- How to use technical indicators to determine where the market, or an individual stock, is headed.
- How to make a trade—I take you through your first day trade, step by step.

- How to manage your money and your emotions.
- And much more, including interviews with professional day traders.

How Much Money Can I Make?

You probably want to know how much money you can make as a day trader. Perhaps you've even set a goal—$200 to $300 a day, for example. Wanting to make money may even be why you're reading this book.

Let me tell you the first goal of this book: it's to help you trade well. Although generating profits is a worthy long-term goal, it's secondary to trading with the odds in your favor, and on probabilities.

Rather than asking, "How much money can I make?" the first question you should ask is, "How much money can I lose?"

Your financial safety is my most important concern, a responsibility I take very seriously. You can make money only if you day trade properly. If you don't, you can lose all of your money faster than you can say, "What happened?"

If you're going to day trade, you must be aware of the risks as well as the benefits. Too many people enter the market with too much money and too little knowledge. In fact, one of the reasons that day trading has a bad reputation is that thousands of people quit their full-time jobs, cashed in their 401(k) accounts, and dumped everything into the market. Many day traders made extraordinary returns, especially at the top of a bull market. Unfortunately, bull markets don't last forever. When they abruptly end, many once successful strategies stop working, and people lose money. Sadly, they sometimes lose more than what they started with.

Remember this: by learning to trade well, you can trade for a lifetime, and not just a day. Therefore, as you read this book, focus on being the best trader you can be. By the time you finish reading, you'll not only learn how to day trade, but also whether day trading makes sense for you and your financial goals.

Making $1,000 per Day

I'll tell you a quick anecdote: I have a friend who was fascinated with how I could enter the market and seemingly pull money out with ease. She assumed the stock market was a huge ATM machine. Once she called me up and said, "I need $1,000. Could you do a day trade for me?"

It reminded me of the nightly infomercials that promise you "$1,000 a day working from the comfort of your own home!"

Nevertheless, consistently making $1,000 a day is possible, but hardly likely, even if you have a $100,000 account. Even $500 a day, or 0.5 percent, would be fantastic. Thousands of professional fund managers would do anything to make those kinds of returns.

My suggestion is to learn about day trading without setting daily financial goals. Start by gaining knowledge and experience. Over time, you'll discover that the key to your success is discipline, a characteristic we'll explore in detail throughout this book.

The Biggest Obstacle to Your Success

Many large institutions spend hundreds of millions of dollars on high-speed computers and complex algorithms to make thousands or more trades per day for pennies to gain an edge over other traders. Those pennies add up to billions of dollars a year. Because so many institutions use these high-frequency strategies, day trading has become more competitive than ever.

Fortunately, the lone day trader can prosper. Although it's not as easy as some people hope, neither is day trading as risky as many think.

If you learn to overcome the biggest obstacle to your success, you can carve out a profitable niche for yourself. That obstacle? Your emotions. Learning how to day trade is the easy part. The hard part is overcoming the psychological challenges. I devote a chapter to this topic, but it could take some time to learn how to ignore your instincts and control your emotions. If there is anything that can damage your account, it's your emotions.

Now that you have a more realistic idea of what you're up against, let's begin. Remember, with the correct information, tools, and mental attitude, you can be a successful day trader.

Chapter 1:
Learning the Business

In this chapter, you'll learn how to open a brokerage account, understand capital requirements, and set up your home office. You'll also learn basic trading information and terminology.

Choosing a Brokerage Firm

After you've decided to day trade, you need to choose a brokerage firm, which is a registered broker-dealer that acts as mediator between buyers and sellers. You must open an account at a brokerage firm to buy or sell stocks.

This important choice involves some careful research. Brokerage firms can be divided into three main types (and all have sophisticated trading platforms and online access):

- Online discount brokerage firms are for self-directed traders, provide little or no investment advice, but offer low commissions, fast execution, sophisticated charting capability, and independent research and customer support.

- Direct-access brokerage firms are similar to online discount brokerages but are usually geared to the professional trader, offering little support to rookies, but low commissions for high-volume traders.
- Full-service brokerage firms primarily work with long-term investors, not day traders. They assign you to work one-on-one with a stockbroker or representative for an annual fee or costly commission, which is the price you pay for investment advice and stock ideas.

Popular online discount brokerage firms include Fidelity Investments, thinkorswim, E*Trade, TD Ameritrade, OptionsXpress, TradeMONSTER, Scottrade, Charles Schwab & Co., and TradeKing, to name a few. Popular direct-access brokerage firms include, Trade Station Securities, MB Trading, and Interactive Brokers, to name a few.

CHOOSING AN ONLINE BROKERAGE FIRM

When you choose an online trading brokerage firm, pick one that has a nationally known reputation, a twelve-hour help desk to answer questions, and competitive commissions (less than $10 per trade).

It's a huge advantage for rookie traders to have a brokerage firm that can answer questions even when the markets are closed. You also want a firm that lets you use a variety of trading strategies (not just buy-and-hold, but day trading or other short-term trading strategies), has easy-to-read charts, and offers timely *fills* (when you buy or sell a stock, the order will be filled, or executed, quickly).

Most online brokerage firms have streaming real-time quotes, easy-to-navigate and secure websites, and understandable profit and loss screens. More than likely, they'll also have competitive commission rates. In addition, the top online brokerage firms have educational resources such as webinars and articles on trading and investing. They may also provide you with built-in trading strategies, the ability to customize charts, set up trading alerts, trade options, and perhaps trade the overseas markets. These perks are usually included with the commissions you pay on trades.

> I highly recommend spending time paper trading before risking real money. Many brokerage firms have paper trading accounts that allow you to practice trading before investing real money into the market. There are also websites that allow you to set up and practice trading without using real money.

To quickly find a reputable online brokerage firm, do an Internet search (suggested search words: "rank online brokerage firms," followed by the current year). A list of articles will appear from independent sources, such as *Smart Money* and other periodicals, that rank brokerage firms. (Rankings from *Barron's* will also appear, but you may have to sign up for a temporary subscription to see them.)

Finally, you can always ask other traders which brokers they recommend. Rookie traders should seriously consider signing up with one of the top online brokerage firms. Why? Because of their excellent reputation, online and phone support, and timely order fills.

USING A DIRECT ACCESS BROKERAGE FIRM

After you've gained experience, you can consider the no-frills direct-access brokers that offer discounts on commissions for high-volume traders. Besides competitive rates, the main advantages of direct access are the customizable charts, the news and scanning data feeds, and very fast fills. Benefits such as fast fills are included in the commissions you pay to trade; others, such as news and data feeds, sometimes require you to pay an additional fee.

Also, by using a direct-access broker, you can manually select an Electronic Communication Network (ECN), a computerized system that allows traders to trade directly with each other. Some traders like to route their orders directly to an ECN, especially in fast markets. Some online brokerage firms allow you to do this as well. The main benefit of using an ECN is the speed.

Lack of customer support is the main disadvantage with some direct-access brokers. Unlike many brokerage firms, who patiently discuss all aspects of trading with you, some direct-access brokers only offer help with their software. The good news? These firms compete fiercely to attract new customers, so many of them are adding more services. Therefore, talk to them to find out exactly what they offer, how much it will cost, and how much support you'll receive.

To find the top-rated direct-access brokerage firms, do an Internet search (suggested search words: "rank direct-access firms," followed by the current year). Again, *Smart Money* and *Barron's* will provide a list of the top direct-access brokers, in addition to other rankings.

Questions, Questions

Before signing up with a brokerage firm, ask a lot of questions, or carefully look at their website. Find out about monthly charges, commissions, and margin rates (the amount of interest you will pay if you borrow money from the brokerage), the kind of chart software they offer, and whether the help desk is open nights and weekends.

If possible, experiment with the trading software and charts before opening an account. Some firms will give you access before you sign up. Brokerage firms highly value active traders like you, so they will try and meet your needs.

Where Do I Sign?

Now that you've chosen a brokerage firm, it's time to open a trading account. Before you're allowed to trade, you must fill out a questionnaire about your trading experience and risk tolerance. Don't be concerned with your answers; it's not a test and it isn't used for anything. (In fact, after you place your first trade, the questionnaire is filed away and, more than likely, never looked at again.)

You'll also learn the minimum requirements to open an account, which may be $2,500, although this will vary depending on the brokerage firm. Then you'll be asked whether you want to open a *margin* or a cash account. Margin simply means that you can borrow money from the brokerage firm, if needed. To give yourself more flexibility, you'll probably want to choose margin, though just because you can use it, it doesn't mean you should. As a beginner, it's best to avoid using margin (for now), but it's helpful to have it available. Nevertheless, it's suggested you learn to trade with your own money before trading with borrowed money.

Note: to be approved for a margin account, you may need a minimum of $5,000. You don't have to provide a credit report to be approved for margin; your collateral is the stocks you're buying.

You'll also be asked to specify the kind of trading style you might use, including day trading. In addition to day trading, you can choose to be an investor or trader. An investor is a person who buys and holds stocks or other financial instruments for an extended time period; a trader, on the other hand, buys and sells stocks or other financial instruments, hoping to profit from short-term price fluctuations. (Eventually, you may consider opening two accounts: one for short-term trading, and another for long-term investments).

Finally, the brokerage firm will ask you how many trades you plan to make per week or month.

However, as soon as you mention day trading, you must follow special rules designed to make sure that you have the financial resources to manage a day trading account. See the section later in this chapter called "What Is a Pattern Day Trader?" to learn about these special rules.

Saving on Commissions

A revolutionary change in the brokerage industry occurred with the move to low commissions. In the old days, brokerages often charged commissions of $100 or more per trade. That forced many people to buy and hold stocks. Once online trading was introduced, expensive commissions became a historical footnote. Now, commissions are usually flat fees of $10 per trade or less, although it varies from firm to firm. You may also be able to negotiate a "per share" commission. It depends on your trading style and the rates charged by your broker.

> For now, stick with paying a flat fee and as you gain experience, you can always explore other commission structures.

Over time, if you do a lot of trading, you can negotiate favorable commissions with the brokerage firm. A professional trader, for example, would probably pay $0.015 or $0.01 per share. Note: even with the lower rates, day trading generates a lot of commissions. To be profitable, you'll need to make more money on the trade than you pay in commissions.

What Is a Pattern Day Trader?

Because of abuses in the past, the National Association of Securities Dealers (NASD) Regulation Board of Directors and the Securities and Exchange Commission (SEC) set up specific guidelines for anyone who day trades. If you make more than four day trades within five business days, you will be designated as a pattern day trader.

For example, if on Monday you buy Oracle (Nasdaq: ORCL) and sell the stock before the end of the day, that is considered a day trade. If you buy Oracle on Tuesday and sell it on Wednesday, that is not a day trade. If you then buy and sell Oracle three times on Thursday, that represents three more day trades, and you've just reached your four day-trade quota. In this example, on Thursday you are now designated as a pattern day trader.

Once you're labeled as a pattern day trader, you must have a minimum of $25,000 in your account at all times. By the end of each trading day, if you don't have $25,000 cash in your account, the brokerage firm can red flag (put a warning) on your account, and even freeze it for ninety days. To be completely safe, you should consider funding your account with $30,000 as a cushion, in case you begin by losing money. Don't blame your brokerage firm; it's the SEC who came up with the rules.

THE FULL-TIME DAY TRADER

Consistently making enough money to support yourself and a family can be a challenge for a full-time trader, even with a $50,000 account. That's why it's important for you to start with a practice account. If you're consistently successful at it, then you might think about trading for a living. However, even though you may not make day trading a full-time career, you can still use some of these strategies when market conditions are right, or even on a part-time basis.

THE PART-TIME DAY TRADER

If you're concerned that you won't be able to come up with the $25,000 minimum required to be a pattern day trader, you have other choices. First, you can plan on being a part-time day trader and not make more than four day trades within five business days. If you choose this strategy, you have to carefully watch your account at all times so you don't make more than four trades in that five-day period.

The main advantage to being a part-time day trader is that you can occasionally use day trading strategies without having to meet the strict financial requirements, such as the $25,000 minimum.

The downside is that it's not easy to stay within the four-trade rule. If market conditions are right, and you see good day-trade set-ups, you may be tempted to add another trade or two, but you can't. If you don't have that $25,000 account, you must not become a pattern day trader. It may be a challenge to limit yourself to fewer than four day trades within five business days, but the alternative is a severe penalty (as mentioned before, your account could be frozen for ninety days). Once you make more than four trades, it's too late: you're a pattern day trader.

The pattern day trader rule involves other nuances, which is why it's best to discuss the requirements with the representatives at the brokerage firm. For example, at this time, IRAs and 401(k)s aren't considered part of the $25,000 minimum. However, many of the rules will likely change over time, so stay current by talking to the representatives. Keep in mind that day trading is not appropriate for your retirement savings. Keep that money separate. Use money you can afford to lose.

Money: Feeling the Pain

If it seems you need a lot of money to make money, consider what professional trader and market wizard William Eckhardt said: "I know of a few multimillionaires who started trading with inherited wealth. In each case, they lost it all because they didn't feel the pain when they were losing. In those formative first few years of trading, they felt they could afford to lose. You're much better off going into the market on a shoestring, feeling that you can't afford to lose. I'd rather bet on somebody starting off with a few thousand dollars than on somebody who came in with millions."

Understanding Margin

If you have a margin account with a brokerage, you may borrow funds from the brokerage firm to finance all or part of a trade. When you do this, there is a margin requirement, meaning that you must have a certain amount of equity (such as cash or securities) on deposit with the brokerage firm to be used as collateral. How much equity you'll need depends on a variety of factors. If you're an investor or trader (not a day trader), the brokerage firm will usually lend you up to 50 percent (depending on the stock you're buying) account value. This is called margin buying power. When you use margin, you are using leverage, which means you are trading with borrowed money. When you use leverage (i.e., margin), although you can increase potential returns, you can also increase the potential losses.

For example, if you had $10,000 and wanted to buy stock, the brokerage firm would likely lend you up to an additional $10,000 to buy more shares. That's a total of $20,000 (2:1 buying power).

Although the brokerage firm has some flexibility in determining how much buying power you have, the Federal Reserve Board sets the maximum amount you can borrow. The exact amount of buying power depends on a number of factors, including the type of security you want to buy and your marginable assets (for example, some assets, such as annuities, are not marginable and can't be used as equity or collateral). Call your brokerage firm to find out the exact rules. In addition, ask the interest rate they charge for margin. More than likely, the interest rate will be quite favorable.

Pattern day traders play by a different, more aggressive set of rules. Once you are designated as a day trader, you will probably be allowed 4:1 *intraday* leverage. For example, if you have $30,000 in the account, you will be given enough buying power to buy a total of $120,000 worth of securities (4 x $30,000). This means total for the day, and not the total you can own at any one time. In other words, you can buy $120,000 worth of securities on Monday, but you're not allowed to hold them overnight. That's because overnight, the margin requirement is still 2:1, which means that if you use all of your intraday buying power (4:1 leverage), you must sell securities before the end of the day to meet the margin requirements (2:1).

If you don't follow these rules, you'll get the dreaded *margin call*. In fact, the last call you ever want to receive is a margin call, which means you must add enough money to your account to meet the margin requirement within twenty-four hours (some brokerage firms give less time, or sometimes more, so be sure to ask), or further action may be taken. For example, they could immediately sell your securities to ensure that the margin call is met.

Bottom line: don't put yourself into a position to receive a margin call. If you do, it's a clear warning signal that you are losing money. This would be a good time to call your brokerage and see if you can work together to protect your account from further damage.

Why Margin Is So Difficult to Manage

Most people, especially beginners, have a difficult time managing margin. In a way, it's like receiving a home equity loan or a credit card with $30,000 down and an additional $90,000 as a loan—very tempting to spend it on a big screen television instead of the new roof you need. For many people, using margin can be an emotional experience since it's so easy to win big or lose big.

> If you're a rookie, I'd recommend not going on margin until you've gained more knowledge and experience. If a trade works in your favor, margin can definitely accelerate the gains. On the other hand, if a trade doesn't work in your favor, the losses can accelerate substantially, and it's possible to damage your account.

In the old days, many uninformed traders used margin to bet huge sums of money on ultimately worthless companies like Pets. com and Kozmo.com. When these companies went bankrupt, so did some traders. It's painful enough to lose money in the stock market, but when you lose borrowed money, it's even worse. Eventually you have to pay back that borrowed money.

If you handle margin properly, and don't use it as an ATM, it can provide you with extra leverage. As a rookie trader, though, you should only buy what you can afford and learn to trade with your own money.

Taxes for Day Traders

Few people want to read much about tax regulations, especially when they change every year. Nevertheless, if you become a full-time trader, you'll need a tax advisor who knows how to handle tax issues. An advisor can also tell you whether it's advantageous for you to use mark-to-market accounting, which is primarily for professionals. This means your securities are revalued at the end of each trading day.

> If you don't trade actively or trade only a small number of shares per trade, hiring a tax advisor could be costly compared to your income from trading. Read IRS Publication 550 (www.irs.gov) for guidance to get you started.

The good news: the Internal Revenue Service (IRS) has improved the way they handle traders' accounts, primarily because trading became so popular and they had to update their methods. Also, brokerage firms have improved their methods of calculating gains and losses. Usually, you'll receive an end-of-year summary that you can simply hand to your accountant. Be sure to hang on to your receipts, as you can deduct certain expenses.

Setting Up a Home Office

Now that you've learned how to open and fund a trading account, the next step is setting up your home office. Although it might be tempting, you don't need to run out to buy a new computer and six monitors.

> Start slowly and don't invest huge amounts of money when setting up your day trading business.

Most traders set up the office in a secluded area of the house so they can concentrate on making serious financial decisions. Install a television set with a mute button (so you can watch but not get distracted by financial networks). Keep it simple at first, and you can always add to it as needed, and as technology improves.

BUYING A DESKTOP COMPUTER

Since your computer can make or break you as a day trader, it's your most important purchase. You'll need enough speed and power to run multiple programs, screens, and news feeds. Day traders must multitask, so you'll need high-speed Internet connections and lots of memory (especially RAM).

No matter what kind of computer you use, be sure it's reliable and fast. Most brokerage firms work best with Windows-based operating systems, but are scrambling to meet the needs of Apple users. Ask your brokerage firm for details on the progress they've made.

Because desktop computers are getting faster and cheaper, standard equipment usually includes large hard drives, graphic cards, multiple ports, and wireless routers. You'll also need to invest in a reliable backup system in case your hard drive fails.

You'll need a high-resolution monitor, which should be at least 19 inches (21 inches is better). This is where you'll put your charts, order entry screens, streaming quotes, and technical indicators. The price of monitors has also dropped, but you should still shop around for a good deal.

Next, you'll need a reliable connection to the Internet. Years ago, installing a high-speed T1 line in your home cost thousands of dollars; now you can connect to your brokerage firm with a DSL or cable modem that's almost as fast as, and a whole lot cheaper than, a T1 line. Fortunately for consumers, prices are far lower than in prior years and speeds keep improving as competition between Internet service providers increases.

Your goal is to trade effectively from home during all market conditions—especially in volatile, fast markets, the kind of environment most day traders crave. It's a personal choice whether to use DSL, cable, or an even newer technology; you just need a dependable, fast connection. Nothing is more frustrating than having to struggle with a slow connection during a fast market. Even worse, you don't want to be knocked offline in the middle of a trade. You may have to experiment with different setups before you make the final decision.

Some traders pay a little more to subscribe to trading newsletters, news feeds, or customized or prebuilt scanning software that helps them choose which stocks to buy or sell. At first, your brokerage firm should meet most of your immediate trading needs. As you become more experienced, you can also pay for additional features (news feeds and scanning software). Again, start slowly and buy only what you really need.

TRADING FROM A LAPTOP COMPUTER

Most professional traders use desktop computers, and perhaps use a laptop in case of emergency or when on vacation. Nevertheless, the newest generation of laptop computers is quite remarkable. The advantage of laptops, obviously, is the freedom to trade anywhere in the world.

In the past, most laptops had extremely small screens, but now some of the largest laptops have plenty of room for your news feeds, order entries, and charts. With a few clicks of the mouse or touchpad, you can see a lot of data. The pros who do trade from a laptop tend to hook up a second 19- or 21-inch monitor to keep tabs on all the information. It's possible to trade from a laptop, but you may have to buy a second, or perhaps a third, high-resolution monitor.

Brokerage firms allow customers to trade on the go, using a variety of mobile devices, including cell phones and tablets. Whether you can make money consistently using these devices is questionable (you may need to see more charts and information than they can show), but they're ideal in emergencies. Without a doubt, there are devices yet to be invented that will make trading on the go even easier.

PROTECTING YOUR COMPUTER

Use a top-of-the-line surge protector to protect your equipment. One errant lightning strike could leave you with a fried computer.

Install the latest virus protection software and—equally as important—Internet security software. It's amazing how many people make financial transactions worth thousands of dollars on unsecured computers with outdated virus software.

Hackers constantly attack vulnerable computers, looking for potential weaknesses. Most brokerage firms spend millions of dollars to protect their online computer accounts from attack, but for a lot less money, you can also protect your home computer. This includes keeping up-to-date with computer patches and system updates, especially if you have a Windows-based system, as they are more prone to viruses. Be sure to have both a physical firewall, most likely built into your router, and a software firewall, included with the Windows software.

If you set up a wireless network at your house, immediately create a strong password so your neighbors or passersby can't piggyback on your Internet connection. Any password should include a combination of letters and numerals.

If you use your laptop outside your home, be wary of using public hotspots when trading stocks. Sophisticated hackers can potentially view pieces of information that you send from your computer to a wireless access point. If you're routinely trading in a remote location, you can buy a broadband card from one of the major cell phone carriers that will give you the most secure connection. If not, stay online for the shortest time possible.

Most important, never use public computers or kiosks when making financial transactions; doing so could put all your account information, including passwords, at risk. Many computers, public or otherwise, are installed with keystroke-logging software that records every transaction you make, including capturing passwords. If you don't follow these basic rules, by the time you return to your hotel or home, your account could be at risk.

What Kind of Trading Strategy Do You Use?

Now that you have a better idea of how to choose a brokerage firm and set up your home office, let's learn more about trading strategies. No one-size-fits-all strategy works for traders. Strategies depend on your personality and trading style. A strategy that works well for one trader may not make any sense to another.

In addition to day trading, you may want to try other trading strategies that have worked well in the past. Of course, past performance doesn't guarantee future results. Nevertheless, there could be times when you'll want to abandon day trading for a more lucrative approach. Here are three of the most recognized trading strategies:

SWING TRADING

Unlike day traders, who rarely hold, or keep, positions overnight, *swing traders* attempt to capture stock gains over a short period of time, typically two to five days. Although not locked into any specific time frame, swing traders usually buy early in the week but are back in cash by the weekend.

Many professional traders use more than one trading style. Therefore, during certain market conditions, they may switch from day trading to swing trading. Swing trading, especially during short-term trending markets, could be the right strategy.

POSITION TRADING

Position traders, unlike day traders or swing traders, hold positions for extended time periods, usually several weeks or months, but possibly longer. Unlike buy-and-hold investors, however, position traders won't hold indefinitely and will sell a position when profits are realized (or to limit losses). In many ways, position trading is similar to swing trading but with a longer hold period.

SCALPING

Before decimalization, scalping was all the rage. That's when traders tried to grab a quick $0.25 per share or more within seconds or minutes, trading thousands of shares, and netting a quick $200 to $500 per trade. It was a lot more difficult than it seemed. At that time, a few popular books written about scalping were misleading—they made scalping sound like an easy strategy that anyone could do, when in fact it is very, very difficult for most people. The practice probably cost people a lot of money.

As a day trader, you will probably scalp on occasion—that is, enter and exit a stock within seconds or minutes for a quick profit. The idea is to make many trades (from five to hundreds) but aim for smaller profits. Keep in mind, however, that this is a stressful trading method that can end in losses because of commissions.

History of the Market

Before the Internet, getting current quotes was a huge ordeal. One hundred years ago, stock quotes were put on blackboards, then communicated to investors and traders by telephone or hired runners. Many people showed up at their broker's office and sat all day staring at blackboards, and, eventually, ticker tape.

The New York Stock Exchange (NYSE), located at 11 Wall Street in Lower Manhattan, opened in 1792 under a buttonwood tree. Twenty-four New York merchants, or stockbrokers, signed the Buttonwood Agreement, which specified they would only trade with each other and which set a fixed transaction fee, later called a commission.

By 1817, the cost of a seat on the exchange was a whopping $25, but ten years later, the cost had risen to $100. (In recent years, a seat on the exchange cost between $3 and $4 million.)

In 1906, the Dow Jones Industrial Average (DJIA) surpassed 100 for the first time in its history. Booms and busts along the way often created millionaires or paupers. For the most part, the public was uninterested in the stock market, considering it a game for the wealthy to play.

That attitude changed in the 1920s, when the public, enthused about the booming stock market, put their paychecks and life savings into the market. It seemed like an easy way for the "little guy" to get rich, and many did. The DJIA peaked at 381 in 1929, a year that will never be forgotten in stock market history.

On October 29, 1929, Black Tuesday, the DJIA plunged, eventually falling to 198. Rumors swirled about suicides of once-wealthy individuals who lost everything. Huge crowds of people gathered around the NYSE, blaming short-sellers for the crash.

A group of bankers, including J.P. Morgan, used their own money to start buying, which temporarily stopped the panic. In fact, the market started going up as people scooped up stocks that seemed like bargains.

Although the next few years saw rallies and corrections, by 1931 the market reached an all-time low of 41, which was 89 percent below its peak. Sadly, it took more than twenty-five years for the stock market to recover its precrash level of 381. By this time the public's taste for the stock market had weakened. Comedian Will Rogers (who may have been quoting Mark Twain) summed up the mood of the country when he said, "I'm not so concerned about the return *on* my money, as the return *of* my money."

Inside the NYSE

Over the next few decades, the NYSE added more trading floors, and installed the latest technology. The NYSE is still considered one of the most prestigious exchanges in the world, and the shares of most of the largest U.S. corporations trade on it. As electronic trading became more common, the NYSE closed its main trading room, as well as other rooms that were no longer needed.

The NYSE specialists, who are responsible for ensuring that all transactions are reported in a timely and accurate manner, have been the heart and soul of the NYSE since its inception. In recent years, the specialists' influence and power has diminished as computers now handle the majority of orders.

Stock or ticker symbols on the NYSE are usually a short abbreviation for the company listed, and are always three letters or fewer. For example, the ticker symbol for Coca-Cola is KO; for General Electric it's GE; for Home Depot, it's HD.

Inside the Nasdaq

The Nasdaq was created in 1971 as the world's first electronic stock market. It exists only electronically and has no trading floor, and thus no people yelling and screaming orders.

At the time it was created, people wondered if a fully electronic exchange was a good idea, but in retrospect, it was ahead of its time. Trading volume on the Nasdaq has continued to increase. In the past, day traders tended to gravitate toward the Nasdaq since it was new and many of the stocks on it were volatile. There, the people who act as middlemen are called *market makers*. They are responsible for providing a two-sided quote (one side for buyers and the other for sellers) for the stocks they handle. One stock may have as many as fifty market makers assigned to it.

A few decades ago the Nasdaq was home to most of the up-and-coming technology stocks. New high-tech companies like Microsoft and Apple were welcomed there because they were too small to be invited to the Big Board (the NYSE).

Nasdaq stock symbols may be four or five letters long. For example, the stock symbol for Intel is INTC, and for Apple, AAPL.

Chapter 2:
Reading Charts

To be a day trader, you'll need a set of powerful tools to help you determine when to enter and exit the market. The most common tool is the stock chart.

When you view a stock chart, you're looking at history: you'll see stock prices moving higher or lower over time. The chart can help you search for statistical clues that may give you an edge over other traders. Using a stock chart means you aren't relying strictly on your emotions to make trading decisions.

Traders say that a picture is worth a thousand words, and you'll see why when you analyze charts. By studying them, you can detect whether buyers or sellers are in control of the market, which can help you find stocks that are on the move, the kind of stocks that can turn into profitable trades.

Stock charts rely on a universal language called *technical analysis*, which is a method of evaluating securities based on price movements and volume. Nearly anyone can understand this language after some study. Technical analysis helps you make statistical assumptions about a stock, which can increase your chances of a successful trade.

When you look at a stock chart, you're primarily looking at price and volume. An alternative method of analyzing stocks is *fundamental analysis*, or the study of the underlying data that affects a corporation. For example, fundamental analysts look at earnings, assets and liabilities, competitive companies, and the actions of company insiders. Some traders use a combination of fundamental and technical analysis, using fundamental analysis to find good companies and technical analysis to determine when to enter or exit.

As a day trader, you'll almost always use technical analysis. When you pull up a stock chart on a screen, you have a choice of time frames ranging from minutes, hours, days, or months. Day traders will use very short time frames: 5-minute, 15-minute, 30-minute, and 60-minute charts. Sometimes they display a daily chart for longer-term trades, and perhaps a weekly chart to identify a longer-term trend.

Chart Basics

Charts are displayed on your computer screen when you sign into your brokerage account. They are constantly updated and have many features, all of which can be customized. Let's take a look at some of the terms you'll repeatedly read and hear about when using technical analysis.

UNDERSTANDING SUPPORT AND RESISTANCE

Support and *resistance* are key concepts in technical analysis, and it's essential that you understand how they work. Basically, as the stock price moves up or down on a chart, it might suddenly slow down or speed up when it reaches support or resistance levels. Understanding support and resistance helps let you know when to enter or exit a position (a stock or any other security).

The concept of support and resistance is actually quite simple: when a stock touches support, which is similar to a floor, it might be a good time to buy (because the price is likely to increase). And when a stock hits resistance, which is similar to a ceiling, it might be a good time to sell (because the price is likely to decrease). Think of support and resistance as a trading zone rather than exact price levels.

To be even more specific, support is the price at which a stock's price has stopped falling and has either moved sideways (e.g., the price is moving in a horizontal pattern) or reversed direction. At this level, selling pressure has dropped off and the demand for the stock was strong enough to prevent the price from dropping further. Demand will exceed supply and prevent the price from falling.

Resistance, on the other hand, is the price at which selling pressure is strong enough to prevent a stock from rising further. Supply exceeds demand, and buying pressure has stopped. More sellers will enter the market and prevent the stock from going higher.

Technicians analyze charts to determine what happens to a stock when it reaches key support or resistance levels. Often, the price of a stock will reverse and bounce off of a support or resistance level. Many day traders take action when a stock breaks through support or resistance.

Whenever you look at a chart, you always want to identify these levels. The key point is determining how the stock, or market, will react when it approaches support or resistance. Will it break through, or will it reverse? To answer this important question, you will probably spend hours studying charts. It is not a skill that can be learned quickly.

Important note: when resistance is broken, that level often turns into support. Conversely, when support is broken, it frequently becomes the new resistance level.

Figure 2.1 is an example of support and resistance (black arrows):

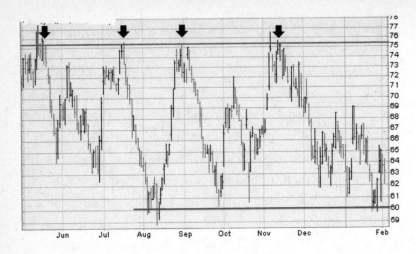

FIG 2.1: Support and Resistance   Source: Stockcharts.com

VOLUME RULES

In conjunction with price, *volume* has always been one of the most important indicators to watch. Volume is simply the number of shares traded over a given period.

Volume is usually displayed at the bottom of a chart. Technicians who study volume observe an incredible amount of information. For example, they'll look to see if a stock, or market, has higher or lower daily volume than in previous days. How is this useful? When you combine volume with price, you will get extremely important clues as to whether the stock (or market) will continue rising or falling, or if it might reverse direction. Like anything related to the stock market, you have to take time to study these clues.

Basically, volume is tabulated by a computer that collects all of the *tick* (price movement) data and draws the volume bars. As volume goes higher, and momentum increases, the volume bars rise. Conversely, as volume decreases, and momentum decreases, the volume bars drop.

To confirm a bullish breakout, technicians want to see if a stock moves higher on higher volume and if the move is accompanied by broad-based buying activity. This is a positive sign for the bulls. On the other hand, a stock falling on higher volume could signal the start of a short-term correction. It is a clue that new buyers are afraid to step in to buy.

What makes a stock go up or down? Buyers push the stock up and sellers push the stock down. A problem with studying volume, however, is that you don't know who is responsible for the increased volume: buyers or sellers. Thus, it's important to use volume to confirm what you see on the chart and not make any trade based only on volume data.

Additionally, the increased popularity of high-frequency trades has skewed some of the volume statistics. For example, a stock may appear to be attracting buying interest, but it's only from high-speed computers scalping for pennies. It's similar to a car stuck in neutral revving its engine: it's making a lot of noise but going nowhere. Again, it's essential you study volume in conjunction with price.

Note: you'll also hear people talk about *liquidity*, which is how easy it is for traders to get into or out of a stock at a single price. Liquid stocks are filled quickly and you can buy or sell them immediately. Illiquid stocks are much more difficult to sell at a competitive price. As you can guess, day traders need liquid stocks in order to get in and out rapidly.

IDENTIFYING THE TREND

The entire purpose of looking at a chart is to help determine which direction the stock is going: up, down, or sideways. Charts help traders identify the trend. By identifying the trend, traders decide whether to follow the trend, wait for a pullback (when the stock price falls back from its peak), or simply stay on the sidelines. One glance at a chart can help determine which direction the stock is currently headed. The challenge, of course, is figuring out when the trend might end.

Let's take a look at the three types of trends: uptrend, downtrend, and sideways.

Making Money on an Uptrend

The popular "follow the trend" strategy has been highly successful for traders over the years. In fact, you may have heard the saying, "The trend is your friend." Nothing is sweeter than buying at the beginning of a trend and riding it until it ends.

When a stock climbs higher and higher, it's on an uptrend. For many traders, following an uptrend is the easiest and most profitable strategy. Sometimes, stocks move up so fast that they "breakout" above the current *resistance* level and move dramatically higher. It's very profitable for traders to own a stock that breaks out.

To be precise, an uptrend occurs when the stock price is making a series of higher highs and higher lows, which you can see on a chart.

For example, when you look at the price pattern on a chart, if today's intraday high (the stock price) is higher than yesterday's intraday high, that's a higher high. A higher low is when today's intraday low is higher than yesterday's intraday low. Multiple higher highs and higher lows makes an uptrend.

Unfortunately, not all markets or stocks cooperate. Although the ideal environment for almost all traders and investors is an uptrend, many markets are choppy and volatile. Day traders, however, can find an uptrend on any chart, from minute to daily charts. As a day trader, you'll primarily use intraday charts such as the 60-minute, 15-minute, and 5-minute to enter and exit trades.

Figure 2.2 is an example of an uptrend:

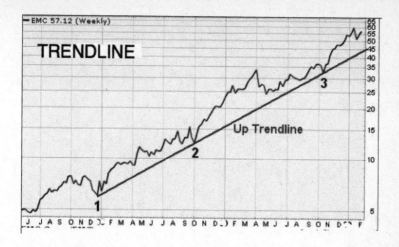

FIG 2.2: Uptrend   Source: Stockcharts.com

Surviving a Downtrend

The opposite of an uptrend is a downtrend, when a stock moves lower and lower. Sometimes stocks will move so low they break down below the current *support* level, and move dramatically lower. It's a money-losing situation if you're long (you bought the stock believing the price would go up) when in a downtrend. To be more precise, a downtrend occurs when the stock price is making a series of lower highs and lower lows. You can see those on the chart.

For example, when you look at the price pattern, if today's intraday low (the stock price) is lower than yesterday's intraday low, that's a lower low. A lower high is when today's intraday high is lower than yesterday's intraday high. Multiple lower lows and lower highs makes a downtrend.

Long, agonizingly slow downtrends, which I characterize as death by a thousand cuts, can be frustrating for investors and traders. Suddenly, in the middle of a downtrend, the market may have a quick, fear-fueled selling frenzy, catching everyone off guard. As a result, stock prices will plunge.

Figure 2.3 is an example of a downtrend:

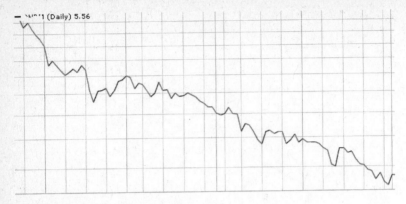

FIG 2.3: Downtrend   Source: Stockcharts.com

Managing a Sideways Pattern

No stock goes up forever, so eventually the stock gets exhausted as sellers overtake buyers. At that point, the stock moves sideways or even falls in price.

You may see a *pattern*, which, according to technical analysts, is simply behavior displayed on a screen. With experience, you'll be able to instantly recognize patterns and perhaps get clues as to what the market, or an individual stock, might do.

The sideways pattern can be very frustrating for traders as the stock goes up and down without going anywhere at all. The sideways trend can last days or weeks, but if you study trends closely, you'll learn there are three types of sideways or horizontal patterns: *trading in a range*, *congestion*, and *consolidation*.

Let's begin by taking a closer look at the three types of sideways patterns.

Trading in a Range

A stock in a trading range can be quite frustrating for some people. A trading range is the difference between the highest and lowest price of a stock. Put another way, a trading range means a stock is moving up and down between support and resistance in a horizontal range. In fact, investors or long-term traders can't seem to generate profits when a stock reaches the top or bottom of a range and reverses direction. In the short term, the stock is moving but doesn't break out of the range. It keeps moving between support and resistance.

As a day trader, if you can identify these reversals, you can make a decent living—but no one said it was easy! Buying when a stock dips and selling when it rallies is a challenging strategy, but it's a skill you must develop if you're serious about being a trader. This is the heart and soul of day trading. It also takes a lot of practice to buy on the dip and sell on a rally when a stock is fluctuating between support and resistance on an intraday chart. Also, on an intraday chart, the trading range is usually a lot tighter than on a daily or weekly chart.

Figure 2.4 is an example of a trading range:

FIG 2.4: Trading Range   Source: Stockcharts.com

Going Nowhere: Congestion

When a stock trades in a range, you can make money when you time it right. But when a stock is in a congestion pattern, it's going nowhere. Author and trader Toni Turner jokingly refers to it as having a stuffed-up nose.

In congestion, the stock fluctuates in a tight, unpredictable pattern that makes trading extremely difficult. In addition, volume is low while in the pattern. Turner gives the following advice: "If you notice stock congestion, stay away. You don't kiss your friends who have colds, and you don't trade stocks that trade in congestion patterns, unless you want your trading account to get sick."

Most traders avoid stocks that are in a congestion pattern, although in this example the stock suddenly broke out of the trading range and moved higher. See **Figure 2.5**.

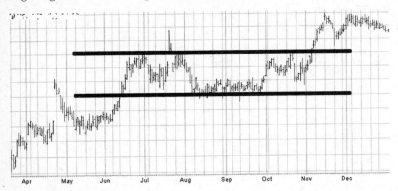

FIG 2.5: Congestion   Source: Stockcharts.com

The Battle: Consolidation

The third sideways pattern is consolidation, which often appears on charts as a very compressed, fluctuating line (if this is hard to visualize, look at Figure 2.6 for an example). Consolidation reflects the battle between buyers and sellers and, when this stock pattern finally ends, it could move violently in either direction, up or down. That is why so many traders like to trade off of this pattern. If you can determine which direction the stock will go, then this pattern will be profitable. The challenge, however, is making a correct prediction. (Hopefully, turning a pattern into a profitable trade will be one of your goals.)

Note: although it is difficult to anticipate if a stock will break above or below a consolidation pattern, there are often clues. For example, look for rising volume, which suggests the stock might make a sudden move. Also, in an uptrend, the stock has a better chance of moving higher out of this pattern. On the other hand, in a downtrend, the stock could suddenly fall.

The longer a stock trades in a consolidation pattern, the more explosive the potential move when it breaks above resistance levels, or below support levels.

Figure 2.6 is an example of consolidation:

FIG 2.6: Consolidation   Source: Stockcharts.com

UNDERSTANDING TIME PERIODS

As mentioned earlier, day traders use short-term time frames such as a 5-minute, 15-minute, 30-minute, 60-minute charts, and a daily chart for a longer-term view. You can also choose weekly or monthly charts to see an even bigger picture. Many day traders will put the major market indexes, such as the Dow, S&P 500, and Nasdaq, on a daily or weekly chart to see the long-term trend. It's a reality check that helps them identify the primary trend. Many traders don't want to go long if the daily trend is down.

The time frame you use when day trading is a personal choice. Experiment until you find your own favorite time frame. For example, Toni Turner likes using an 8-minute chart, while other traders often use a 5-minute or 10-minute chart. "I like to use 8-minute charts for day trading," Turner says, "in place of the 5-minute charts that most traders use. I like to 'get off the fives' because most other traders are on 5-, 10-, or 15-minute charts. I also use 13-minute charts. I use daily charts to target the primary trend, support and resistance, and entry price. Then I drill down to my intraday charts to execute entries."

> No matter what time frame you choose, 10-minute, 60-minute, or daily, always look at the stock over a span of days. If you're looking at a 10-minute chart, look at it over a period of two to three days. You want to see if the stock is climbing above the previous day's high, or whether it's weak compared with yesterday. A month is probably too long if you're day trading, a few days is recommended.

Chart Types

Now that you have a basic understanding of chart vocabulary, we'll take a closer look at the three most popular chart types. When you pull up a chart, you choose which type you want to view: line, bar, or candlestick. There are advantages and disadvantages to each, which we will discuss.

EASY ON THE EYES: LINE CHARTS

In the past, many Western traders relied on two-dimensional line charts to get a visual snapshot of the stock market. A line chart simply plots the closing prices of a stock over a specific period. Then a line connects each price point.

They're the easiest to use and are visually appealing, especially when seen on television, PowerPoint presentations, or in books. Although long-term investors or traders sometimes use line charts for a "big picture" view of the market, line charts don't provide much detailed information.

> Bottom line: day traders usually need more information than a line chart can provide.

Figure 2.3 is an example of a line chart.

MORE DETAILS: BAR CHARTS

A bar chart provides more details about the market open, close, high, and low. A bar chart includes a horizontal scale at the bottom of the chart with a range of prices for almost any time period. The "bar" is the stock's price range for the time period.

In a daily chart, for example, the top of the bar represents the highest price sold for the day, while the bottom of the bar represents the lowest price for the day.

Each bar also has a short horizontal line that extends to the left and to the right. The left line represents the opening price for the trading day, and the right line marks the closing price. By studying a bar chart in combination with volume, astute traders can get clues as to who is in control of the market: buyers or sellers.

> Bottom line: bar charts are more useful than line charts, but day traders probably want to use the next chart type: candlesticks. This can really help you read the mind of the market.

SEEING WHO'S IN CONTROL: CANDLESTICK CHARTS

Day traders need even more information than is provided by line or bar charts, which is why candlestick charts are so popular. They show the range between the opening and closing price of a stock during any given time period.

With one glance at a candlestick, experienced traders can immediately see whether the bulls or bears are in control, and whether a reversal is possible. When used in conjunction with traditional *technical indicators* (formulas displayed on a chart to determine a stock's, or other security's, future price movements), candlesticks can be a powerful source of information. With a little experience, candlesticks are also relatively easy to interpret. Toni Turner put it this way: "Candlestick charts are the luxury version of bar charts. It's like switching from a black-and-white television set to living color."

> Bottom line: it's recommended that you use candlestick charts because they provide a vast amount of information and visual clues.

Figure 2.7 is a daily candlestick chart of the S&P 500.

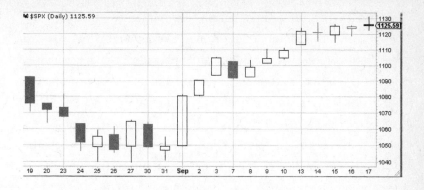

FIG 2.7: Candlestick 1 Month   Source: Stockcharts.com

The History of Candlesticks

Candlesticks are actually the oldest form of technical analysis, originally created by Munehisa Homma, a wealthy Japanese rice trader, in the eighteenth century. Steve Nison, president of Candlecharts.com and author of the best-selling book, *Japanese Candlestick Charting Techniques* (Prentice-Hall, 2001), was the first to introduce candlesticks to the West.

"The Japanese say that every candlestick line tells a story," Nison says. "The candlestick has the same information as the bar chart but it's constructed differently. By using candlesticks, you can visually see who's in control of the market at the time the candlestick is formed."

Real Body

The candlestick has two main components, the *real body* and *shadows*. The real body is the rectangular portion of the candlestick and displays the range between the opening price of the stock and its closing price. With a quick glance of the real body, you can gain clues as to whether the bulls or bears are in control of the market.

Studying the color of the real body gives important information. If the real body is white (or clear), it simply means the close was higher than the open, a bullish sign. The taller and longer the white real body, the more bullish it is. During a rally, you want to see a series of long white candles, and preferably on higher volume.

On the other hand, a black (or filled in) real body means the close was lower than the open. The taller and longer the black real body, the more bearish it is. A series of long black candles can indicate the bears are now in control. "We get nervous when the real body gets smaller and smaller because it means that supply and demand is becoming more equal," Nison explains.

Put another way, long white candlesticks reflect strong buying pressure while long black candlesticks reflect strong selling pressure. Short candlesticks reflect that prices are consolidating, i.e. not moving too far in one direction or another.

Shadow

The *shadows* of a candlestick are the thin lines that jut out above or below the real body. Shadows reflect the highs or lows of the day. The shadow above the real body is the upper shadow, while the shadow below is the lower shadow. For example, a long upper shadow indicates that the day's high was well above the open and the close. Conversely, a long lower shadow indicates that the day's low was well below the open and the close. It gives traders a clue as to whether buyers or sellers are in control. Therefore, a candlestick with a long upper shadow and short lower shadow indicates that buyers are in control; prices went higher. Conversely, candlesticks with long lower shadows and short upper shadows indicate that sellers are in control and therefore prices went lower.

Open and Close

As you gain more experience, it will be clear that the most important part of each day is the open and close. Traders are often quite emotional when placing their orders at the open. The last hour is also volatile, as many traders close their positions.

To review, the top of the candlestick body represents the closing price, and the bottom is the opening price. If the candle body is hollow or white, the closing price was higher than the opening price. Conversely, if the candle body is black, the closing price was lower than the opening price. With one glance you can discover detailed information about the security.

Drawing Trendlines

Did you ever play the game, "Connect the Dots?" This is exactly what it's like when you draw trendlines. (Instead of dots, however, you connect a series of highs and lows on a chart to confirm a trend.) Drawing trendlines helps you to determine support and resistance. This can help determine when to enter a stock, or when to exit.

You can use your brokerage firm's software to draw trendlines or, if you want to do it the old-fashioned way, take out a ruler and connect the highs and lows.

If you draw two trendlines, one connecting the highs and one connecting the lows, you will create what analysts call a *channel* (or *envelope*). Creating a channel can help you determine price targets (a projected price), which is based on the concepts of support and resistance.

By drawing trendlines, you'll be able to see on a chart when a stock or index is making higher highs and higher lows (uptrend). Conversely, you can also see if a stock is making lower lows and lower highs (downtrend). In both examples, an increase in volume boosts uptrends and downtrends. You can look at the volume bars to see if volume is supporting the move higher or lower.

Figure 2.2 shows a trendline in an uptrend. Notice how the trendline, which acts as support (which is like a floor), connects to the three low points (#1, #2, and #3).

Chapter 3: Interpreting Patterns

You can look at chart patterns to find stocks to buy or sell, though as a rookie day trader, patterns may be one of the last tools you'll need to study. It does take practice to interpret them correctly. Some rookie traders make a few trades based on patterns only to watch them fail, and give up. That's why you don't want to make a trade based solely on one pattern. Instead, use technical indicators to confirm what you think you see.

Some traders immediately see the patterns, while others look but don't notice anything. In fact, if you're good at pattern recognition, you'll want to explore the dozens of other patterns that you'll see on charts. I've included a list of additional sources in the Resources appendix if you want to learn more.

If patterns aren't your strongest area, memorize only the most important ones (such as those included in this chapter). Fortunately, the more you study charts, the more you'll be able to recognize the patterns. If you're keeping a trading journal to record your trading experiences (a practice I highly recommend), be sure to keep track of the patterns that work for you, and the ones that don't.

Let's begin by taking a look at the key patterns that are most useful to day traders. Many of these chart patterns will be used on very short time frames such as on a 5-minute, 30-minute, or 60-minute chart.

Basic Chart Patterns

These chart patterns are the most popular ones used by day traders. As mentioned earlier, making trades based on patterns can be difficult and, as a rookie, it won't be your highest priority. That being said, it's useful to learn the most basic patterns in case you do see them on a chart.

DOUBLE BOTTOM (BULLISH)

A common bullish reversal pattern is the double bottom, which looks like a "W." After an extended downtrend, the stock has failed to break through support after two attempts, and rallies higher. After the pattern is complete, the trend changes from bearish to bullish.

There is always the chance, however, that the stock will consolidate, or stagnate, before breaking through resistance and moving higher. Look for an early increase in volume on the left bottom before the first breakout. Although this is an easily recognized pattern, the double bottom doesn't always give an actionable signal, so be sure to confirm with other technical indicators before you make a trade based on this pattern.

Figure 3.1 is what the double bottom pattern looks like:

FIG 3.1: Double Bottom   Source: Stockcharts.com

DOUBLE TOP (BEARISH)

The double top, which looks like an "M," is a major bearish reversal pattern that shows two peaks at the same price level. After an uptrend, the stock has failed to break through resistance after two attempts. After the pattern is complete, the trend changes from bullish to bearish.

There is always the chance the stock will move sideways before it breaks through support and moves much lower. Look for an increase in volume near the left top before the stock heads lower. One of the most famous double tops was the Nasdaq in 2000, and anyone who paid attention to the signal probably saved his or her portfolio.

Just as with the double bottom, the double top is easily recognizable but doesn't always give an actionable signal. As always, you'll want to confirm with technical indicators before you make a trade based on this pattern.

Figure 3.2 is what the double top pattern looks like:

FIG 3.2: Double Top   Source: Stockcharts.com

HEAD AND SHOULDERS (BEARISH)

The head and shoulders reversal pattern shows up a lot in charts, indicating that buying has stopped at the top of the trend, and has the potential to reverse direction. If you look at the chart in **Figure 3.3**, you'll see that the stock really does look like a head and shoulders.

The stock moves higher, then pulls back to form the left shoulder. It then moves higher to form the head, but fails to break through support, forming the neckline. Finally, the stock rises again to form the right shoulder, but fails to break resistance. At this point, this pattern tells us that the stock is doomed as it falls below the neckline.

In addition to watching the price, you'll also study volume. Generally, the head is formed on diminished volume indicating that buying pressure is not as strong as the first move upward on the left shoulder. Volume should decrease on the right shoulder for the pattern to play out. On the last attempt in the right shoulder, volume should be even less than the head, indicating that buying volume has disappeared.

> An inverted head and shoulders, which is bullish, is the exact opposite of the head and shoulders.

Figure 3.3 is what the head and shoulders pattern looks like (#1 and #2 are the low points):

FIG 3.3: Head and Shoulders   Source: Stockcharts.com

GAPS

A gap occurs when a stock opens up at a different price from where it closed the previous day. For example, if Microsoft closed at $23.80 on Wednesday and then opens at $24.55 on Thursday, there would be a $0.75 gap in the chart. Gaps, which show up as open spaces on a chart where no trading has occurred, are the result of an imbalance between buy and sell orders.

Gaps are caused by breaking news or earnings reports, or because there's no trading at a particular price level. When this occurs, the stock suddenly jumps, reflecting strong buying or selling pressure in the stock.

Gaps show up most frequently in a daily chart, but you may see them when trading intraday. An intraday gap almost always occurs with stocks that are thinly traded. In a normal stock that does a decent amount of volume, an intraday gap doesn't occur often (exception: a midday breaking news report). Most gaps occur in the premarket or postmarket.

Sometimes you'll hear traders talking about "filling the gap," which simply means that the price will *retrace*, or go back, to the last price before the gap, resulting in the gap being closed. In the example above, Microsoft would fill the gap by retracing to $23.80.

There are actually four types of gaps:

Common Gaps

These uneventful gaps appear relatively often, perhaps caused by an order imbalance. More than likely, volume will be relatively low and the gap is filled, or closed, rather quickly. Common gaps often occur when a stock is moving sideways. A common gap probably won't give you a trading opportunity, especially if volume is low. Most technicians advise not trading them at all.

Figure 3.4 is what a common gap looks like:

FIG 3.4: Common Gap   Source: Stockcharts.com

Breakaway Gaps

The breakaway gap can be the most profitable and exciting if you own shares before it breaks out. Suddenly, the stock gaps up, perhaps on higher than normal volume. This may be the start of a significant move higher, or so the bulls hope.

It's possible that the stock will continue to move higher on strong volume in the same direction as the gap. Although the gap may eventually be filled, it may not happen immediately, which is why traders like breakaway gaps. In fact, it could take a long time to fill.

Some professional traders like to buy breakaway gaps right at the open (not recommended for rookies because stock prices sometimes fall quickly at the open. If you are riding a breakaway gap, you probably *don't* want to take your profits right away, especially if you are long the stock overnight. Why? This could be the start of a new trend higher. Therefore, assuming you have profits at day's end, you'll probably change from being a day trader to a swing trader. Again, no one said that trading was easy!

Figure 3.5 is what a breakaway gap looks like:

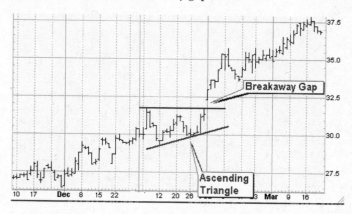

FIG 3.5: Breakaway Gap   Source: Stockcharts.com

Runaway or Continuation Gap (Also Referred to as Measuring Gap)

Just as with the breakaway gap, the runaway gap suddenly gaps up on higher volume and increased enthusiasm from buyers. Sometimes there will be a sudden pullback before the stock breaks out and continues upward. It is as if the stock pauses or rests before resuming its prior trend.

You may wonder what the difference is between a breakaway gap and a runaway gap. According to technicians, the runaway gap occurs in the middle of a trend, while the breakaway gap begins a new trend. Don't worry if you find it hard to distinguish between the various gaps; it definitely takes experience to trade them successfully. With much more experience, you'll eventually learn the nuances of using gaps, and perhaps when to detect profitable opportunities. Simple? No. Possible? Yes.

Figure 3.6 is an example of a runaway gap:

FIG 3.6: Runaway Gap   Source: Stockcharts.com

Exhaustion Gaps

Eventually, all good gaps come to an end. After the stock has made its move higher and higher, the stock suddenly gaps up on higher than normal volume. Then, late in the trend, after the big price move, the stock gets exhausted, and demand decreases. A correction may be imminent. The stock will slow down as the stock price falters. Because exhaustion gaps are often followed quickly by a reversal, informed traders immediately enter sell orders as they realize the gap is ending, so there could be a mad dash out of the stock.

In addition, volume may pick up as previous buyers notice the exhaustion and unload their shares. Hopefully you are already out of the stock before it reverses, because now it may feel like it's too late to get out.

Figure 3.7 is an example of an exhaustion gap:

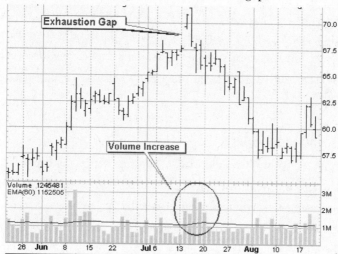

FIG 3.7: **Exhaustion Gap**   Source: Stockcharts.com

Chart Patterns for Experienced Traders

Now that you've been introduced to the most basic patterns, it's time to step it up a notch. The following patterns aren't that difficult to spot, but turning them into a profitable trade takes skill and experience.

Learning how to identify these patterns can be useful, but don't worry if you can't "see" some of them. Simply draw trendlines to make them more visible. Most chart programs allow you to draw lines, which makes patterns easier to recognize.

TRIANGLES

One common pattern is a triangle, which is part of a *continuation* pattern. To refresh your memory, a continuation pattern means the stock is simply continuing to move in the same direction, perhaps pausing (*consolidating*) along the way, but the stock trend remains intact. The continuation pattern can be bullish or bearish, but the trend is not disrupted.

There are three main types of triangles: *ascending*, *descending*, and *symmetrical*. With a little practice, you'll start seeing triangles everywhere!

Ascending Triangles

In an ascending triangle, the stock price is making higher lows, but the highs remain the same, indicating that resistance is strong in that area. Nevertheless, every time that price sells off from the resistance level, away from that area, bulls are willing to step in earlier and earlier to buy, thereby creating the ascending triangle pattern. A breakout is inevitable where the two lines converge. As the point of the triangle is formed, the lower line of the triangle acts as support while the upper line of the triangle acts as resistance.

Figure 3.8 is an example of the ascending triangle, a bullish pattern.

FIG 3.8: Ascending Triangle (Bullish)   Source: Stockcharts.com

Descending Triangle

The descending triangle is an inverted image of an ascending triangle. A descending triangle is making a decline to a new low. Every time the stock tries to rally, bears are willing to step in earlier and earlier, trying to sell the stock, thereby creating the descending triangle pattern. Where the two lines converge, it's possible there will be a downside breakout. Again, as the point of the triangle is formed, the lower line of the triangle acts as support while the upper line of the triangle acts as resistance.

Figure 3.9 is an example of a descending triangle, a bearish pattern.

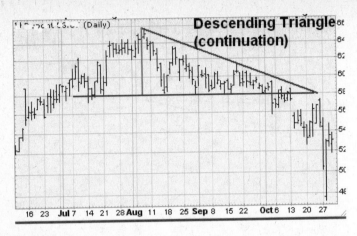

FIG 3.9: Descending Triangle (Bearish)   Source: Stockcharts.com

Symmetrical Triangles

Small symmetrical triangles are called *flags* and *pennants*. Many traders claim that flags (and pennants) are some of the most reliable signals. (Unfortunately, technical analysis is not 100 percent accurate, but some patterns are more reliable than others.) Continuation patterns such as flags and pennants allow a stock to rest by moving sideways for a while before continuing to trend higher or lower. "It's the pause that refreshes," some traders jokingly say.

Pennants

Keep in mind that a *pennant* is similar to a small triangle, but its trendlines converge as the pattern is formed. Ideally, there will be a strong move, up or down, after the pattern is completed, and the lines narrow, which creates the pennant.

Flags

Flags are short-term continuation patterns that reflect a brief pause (consolidation) after a quick move, before taking off again. You'll want to see if volume increases as the pattern is being formed.

Although similar to a pennant, a flag's trendlines are nearly parallel. When you see this pattern on a chart, it really looks like a flag (and it often has a mast on either side)!

Figure 3.10 is an example of a bull flag:

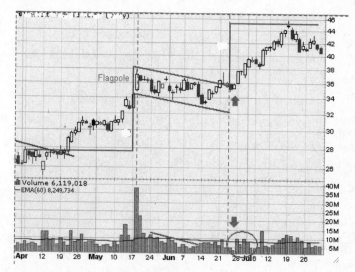

FIG 3.10: Bull Flag   Source: Stockcharts.com

Note: A bear flag, on the other hand, looks like an inverted flag on a flagpole.

Candlestick Patterns

Many traders look at candlestick pattern formations for clues to when to buy or sell. Candlesticks are often used to gain clues to market psychology or changes in the trend.

Here are a few of the most popular candlestick patterns:

THE DOJI

The doji is a very common candlestick pattern characterized by small, thin lines and an equal opening and closing price. The cross formed is the doji, which is often interpreted as indecision between the bears and the bulls. If you see a stock that makes a doji top, after confirming with other indicators, you might think about taking money off the table. The doji is a definite warning signal.

In addition, there are variations of the doji, such as the gravestone doji (open and close occur at the low of the day, which signals a major turning point in the direction of the trend) and the long-legged doji (open and close are nearly equal, which signals indecision).

DARK CLOUD COVER

The dark cloud cover is another common candlestick pattern thought to be quite reliable. It's most useful at identifying market tops. Looking as if it's a cloudy day, this pattern often shows that buyers are giving up and sellers are becoming more aggressive.

HAMMER

The hammer, a bullish reversal pattern, has a short real body that's at the top of that day's trading range. When you see it for the first time, it really does look like a hammer!

Often the hammer will form at the end of a stock advance, in which case it's a *hanging man*. When the hammer forms at the end of a stock decline, it is called a *bottoming tail hammer*.

HOW TO USE CANDLESTICK PATTERNS

Steve Nison, president of Candlecharts.com and a candlestick pattern expert, shared his insights about the use and misuse of candlestick charts. One of the most common candlestick patterns, Nison says, is the *bearish engulfing pattern*, "when the black real body wraps around the white real body. This has more likelihood of a reversal than the dark cloud cover."

But even more reliable, he says, is when a candlestick pattern confirms a traditional Western pattern. "You can use candlesticks to confirm the pattern, and have a greater likelihood of a trade working out," Nison notes. "For example, you could use the dark cloud cover to confirm resistance, which is a stronger signal than a dark cloud cover by itself."

The key is to understand that candlesticks reflect market psychology. Therefore, he suggests that you focus on the patterns that make the most sense to you. "You'll find a lot of doji patterns on a chart," he says, "but because they are so frequent, they are not as important on an intraday chart."

One of the advantages of candlesticks, Nison adds, is "that it shows the force of the current move. For example, if you have a hammer at the bottom end of a recent downtrend, the candlestick will show that less of that downtrend is losing momentum."

What is important for day traders, he says, is studying the individual candle lines for signals. "If you have a series of hammers, a series of lower shadows at the same support area, it's showing you either demand is coming in or supply is drying up."

Although there are dozens of actionable candlestick signals, Nison uses scanning software to focus in on only the twenty patterns that make the most sense for him. If you are first learning about candlesticks, he recommends having an even smaller list.

MISUSES OF CANDLESTICKS

Not surprisingly, some traders misuse candlesticks. "A lot of people see the doji and think there will be a reversal," Nison notes. "A doji during an uptrend means the market has gone from up to neutral. It doesn't mean it's gone from up to down. It's increasing the likelihood of a reversal but it doesn't make it 100 percent." The key to being an informed trader, he suggests, is getting a candlestick education.

Another example of candlestick misuse is the hammer candle signal. "You might have a hammer signal that you shouldn't buy. Then again, you could have a hammer signal that might be a great buying opportunity. We call that a candle in context. Look at the candle in the prism of the current market action." For example, he'd combine technical concepts such as support and resistance and overall market direction with candlestick signals.

"If the hammer is within a longer-term trend, however you define it," he explains, "and the hammer is confirming a support level, and if there is a good risk-reward on the trade, I'd be more aggressive at buying than a hammer that is within a longer-term downtrend."

Other misuses of candlesticks include using them by themselves without technical indicators, and not paying attention to money management before placing a trade. In particular, Nison says it's essential that you use stop-loss orders.

"I place my stops using candle signals, for example, under the low of the hammer," Nison says. "I prefer to wait for the market close, but if you're trading intraday and you can't wait for the close, you have to place certain intraday stops."

It's sometimes too late for day traders to wait for the market close, so you have to place intraday stops. Nison explains, "I use the candle to set stopout levels, for example, the high of the shooting star, the high of the doji, or the low of the hammer, or the low of the bullish engulfing pattern."

It's very important, Nison suggests, to first determine if a trade has a favorable risk-reward. "You could have a great candle signal," he says, "but if it's not a good risk-reward, the candlestick doesn't matter."

He cautions that one of the biggest problems with candlesticks is that people recognize a pattern and immediately buy. "Even if you have a candlestick signal, you should confirm with Western technicals," Nison explains. "The mistake that people make is relying solely on candlesticks. You shouldn't look at them in isolation."

In fact, one of the limitations of candlesticks is that they don't give price targets. "Candlesticks are good at picking highs and lows, and helping know when to exit," says Nison, "but you need Western technical analysis to get price targets. This is why our education focuses on the best of candlesticks with the best of Western indicators."

ADVICE FOR DAY TRADERS

Nison suggests that day traders keep their eye on the daily charts even if they're not trading them. "If you have support and resistance on a daily chart," he says, "that's usually more important than support and resistance from the intraday charts, since most people are looking at daily charts. So I would keep a daily chart in the back of my mind when day trading to see if I get any candlesticks that confirm the support and resistance levels."

For example, if support is at $20 on a daily chart, and you see a bullish hammer or bullish engulfing pattern, Nison says that's more significant than the bullish engulfing pattern confirming support on an intraday chart. The reason? The daily chart has a longer time frame, which is more significant.

On the other hand, one of the advantages of looking at an intraday chart is you sometimes get an early reversal signal, Nison says. "Let's say in the first two hours of trading on an intraday chart you see a bullish engulfing pattern," he says. "By the end of the day on the daily chart, the market might have moved up already, so by the time you get the candle signal, it's too late."

He explains that the candle signal on a daily chart needs the close of the day, while on a 30-minute chart, for example, all you need is the close of the 30-minute period. "Even if you are swing trading, look at the intraday charts for an early turning signal," Nison suggests.

Nison has some final advice for traders: "I have seen traders lose lots of money with the wrong information about candlesticks. It is vital that if you really want to use candlesticks correctly, it's essential you get the right information."

The Contradictory History of Level II

Level II, a Nasdaq data feed provided either free or for a small monthly charge by most brokerage firms, shows quotes from the Nasdaq market makers. When you type in a symbol for a Nasdaq stock in Level II, you'll see the market participants sorted by the best bid and ask prices (the bid price is the highest price a buyer is willing to pay for a stock, and the ask price is the lowest price a seller is willing to accept for a stock).

Years ago, Level II was extremely popular with traders. It gave market players an inside look at what the market makers were up to, or what is called market depth. Day traders were particularly interested in Level II, gaining insights into market action that helped give them an edge.

Entire books were written about using Level II to make money by scalping. Traders closely studied Level II for clues, trying to identify who was "The Ax," or the market maker who controlled all the orders on a particular stock. One strategy included emulating the trades of the Ax, who was usually on the right side of a trade.

But the rules changed, first moving from fractions to decimalization. Then market makers who posted prices on Level II were allowed to hide their true size, so a 10,000-share order may show 100 shares. Another trick was placing an imaginary 50,000-share sell order to scare away other market players from placing buy orders.

Although Level II is not as popular as in the past, many traders still find it valuable to discover the most competitive prices. Others use it to find support and resistance. For example, if you see a cluster of colors at a certain price level, this could be used for support or resistance. All that congestion gives traders an idea where to place their stops.

If you're curious about Level II, ask your brokerage firm for access. Some provide it at no cost, and others charge a small monthly fee.

While Level II quotes have both proponents and critics, many traders find that the information found in Time and Sales, another feature added to Level II, to be very useful. Time and Sales displays the actual trades (or *prints*) that are taking place. In addition to the price, it shows the size of the order and the true time the trade was made.

Unlike Level II, where orders are often hidden, Time and Sales shows orders executed on an exchange. This represents *most* of the orders. (Why not all orders? It has been reported that anonymous, large orders are sometimes arranged "off the books.")

Nevertheless, Time and Sales tells traders what's really happening in the market. For example, if you see a stock rallying, and Time and Sales verifies there is a surge of large trades, it's a clue that bigger players are in the game.

Keep in mind that, although traders do look at Time and Sales for clues, it's only another tool to help determine market strength, not a definitive answer. Although useful for many, only you can determine if it's worthwhile for you.

Figure 3.11 is a screen display of Time and Sales:

MSFT   Go ▾ Trade Hide Quote

Real-Time | Historical

MSFT   MICROSOFT CORPORATION

Last **23.96** ↑   -0.33   Bid **23.96**   Size **9**   Ask **24.09**   Size **50**

Time	+	Last Price	Last Size	Last Exch	Bid Price	Bid Size	Bid Exch	Ask Price	Ask Size	Ask Exch	Trade Cond
19:59:17		23.98	300	Q	23.98	223	Q	24.00	26	Q	T
19:43:34		23.98	200	Q	23.98	228	Q	24.00	26	Q	
19:17:32		24.00	800	Q	23.98	228	Q	24.00	34	Q	
18:41:55		23.98	200	Q	23.97	17	Q	24.00	34	Q	
18:30:01		23.98	420	Q	23.97	17	Q	23.99	4	Q	
18:17:19		24.00	2000	Q	23.96	9	P	24.00	50	Q	
18:11:12		23.96	8900	DF	23.98	15	Q	24.01	2	Q	T
18:11:07		23.96	27034	DF	23.98	15	Q	24.01	2	Q	T
18:03:41		24.01	2822	Q	23.99	8	P	24.01	2	Q	T
18:03:41		24.01	900	Q	23.99	8	P	24.01	40	Q	T
18:03:37		24.00	100	P	24.00	6	P	24.01	40	Q	T
18:03:37		24.00	100	Q	23.99	8	P	24.00	1	Q	
17:56:01		23.99	100	AL	23.97	7	Q	24.00	2	Q	T
17:53:57		23.99	250	Q	23.97	7	Q	24.01	40	Q	
17:51:34		23.99	300	P	23.99	7	Q	24.00	3	P	
17:50:24		23.98	100	Q	23.98	1	Q	24.00	3	P	T
17:47:15		23.99	100	P	23.98	1	Q	23.99	1	P	
17:47:15		23.99	100	Q	23.98	1	Q	23.99	1	P	
17:37:05		23.96	100	P	23.96	9	P	23.99	10	P	T
17:37:05		23.96	600	P	23.96	9	P	23.99	10	P	T
17:37:04		23.96	300	P	23.96	9	P	23.99	10	P	T
17:37:02		23.96	700	P	23.96	13	P	23.99	10	P	T
17:37:02		23.96	900	P	23.96	13	P	23.99	10	P	T
17:37:02		23.96	400	P	23.96	13	P	23.99	10	P	T
17:37:00		23.96	500	P	23.96	18	P	23.99	10	P	
17:36:59		23.96	1100	P	23.96	18	P	23.99	10	P	T
17:36:59		23.96	900	P	23.96	18	P	23.99	10	P	T
17:36:54		23.96	100	P	23.96	38	P	24.00	3	P	
17:36:54		23.96	777	P	23.96	38	P	24.00	3	P	

FIG 3.11: Time and Sales   For illustrative purposes only. Source: Fidelity Investments.
© 2010 FMR LLC. All rights reserved. Used by permission.

Chapter 4:
Using Technical Indicators

As you learn more about day trading, you will rely more and more on a set of tools called technical indicators, which are those crooked little lines plotted on, above, or below a stock chart. They measure a stock's short-term price activity in various ways to help predict the stock's future price movement. You usually select indicators from a dropdown list that is next to the chart. They are used to help increase the odds of making a successful trade. Many day traders use technical indicators to make trading decisions.

For example, one use of indicators is to help identify when the market or an individual security is *overbought* or *oversold*. When there is too much buying (overbought), or too much selling (oversold), this is a clue there could be a reversal. Why? Because if a stock or index has risen too much and too quickly, a pullback often occurs. Identifying overbought and oversold conditions is just one way to use technical indicators.

Some traders use technical indicators to try and predict, or anticipate, stock or index direction. Although indicators are helpful, don't make the common mistake of letting them make the buying and selling decisions for you. Indicators provide important information about market conditions, but in the end, you make the trading decision. You have to put all of the pieces together to make a diagnosis.

Although there are hundreds of technical indicators, many are too slow to be useful to day traders. That's why I'll focus on a set of indicators that are popular with many day traders. Eventually you'll find a handful of indicators that make sense to you and your trading methodology.

If you've never used indicators before, this chapter may seem a little overwhelming at first. After you've used indicators a few times, however, you'll find they're easy to put on a chart (but not always easy to interpret). If you want to learn even more about technical indicators, you can pick up a copy of my book, *All About Market Indicators* (McGraw-Hill, 2011), which was written for the novice trader.

Finding Indicators That Work for You

Although you'll soon be introduced to a number of indicators, you don't want to have more than four or five on a chart at one time. Some traders use so many indicators they get afflicted with a condition known as "indicatoritis," as one financial blogger put it.

Unfortunately, there is no magic indicator that will give you all the answers. Indicators simply guide you in the right direction, pointing out clues as to what may occur. At times, indicators contradict each other, so you must act as a referee and determine which is giving the right message. For example, one indicator may generate a buy signal, while another indicator may generate a sell signal. Often, some indicators work well in one market environment but not well in another. For example, moving averages (MA) work well in a trending environment but are not as effective in a choppy market.

The indicators you'll read about next should not be considered as actionable trades, but only guidelines. Also, always use other indicators to confirm before buying or selling a stock or index.

The Most Popular Indicator: Moving Averages

Moving averages are one of the most popular technical indicators, and often the most reliable, no matter what your time frame. To be specific, moving averages show the value of a security's price over the duration of a time period, for example, the last 20, 50, 100, or 200 days. When you overlay the moving average over the stock price, the relationship between the moving average and price is visible. Again, the experienced eye may be able to discern valuable clues about how the stock price may react.

Moving averages are easy to understand and, when interpreted properly, can result in profitable trades. When moving averages are plotted, trends (discussed earlier) can be quickly identified. Most important, moving averages often signal when a trend may begin, or end. The two most common moving averages are the *simple* moving average (SMA) and the *exponential* moving average (EMA).

THE SIMPLE MOVING AVERAGE

Many people use the simple moving average because it's the default on most chart programs.

A 10-day simple moving average, for example, is calculated by taking an average of the last 10 days of the stock's closing price and dividing by 10. So, as the tenth day is added, the first day is dropped off. In other words, old days are dropped as new days become available.

Moving averages constantly move. As the procedure is repeated every day, a smooth line is created that can be displayed on a chart. The longer the time frame, the more powerful the signal, another reason why even day traders need to study multiple time frames. Why is a 5-day MA more powerful than a 1-day MA? More data are used in the calculation, so it's timelier. In addition, a 60-minute chart is more powerful than a 5-minute chart.

As a day trader, you'll use short time frames: minutes and hours. Knowing what happens over several days will be useful, but will not necessarily affect your intraday trades. Fortunately, moving averages are flexible enough to be used on nearly any time period, including intraday. By the way, when looking at moving averages on an intraday chart, the vocabulary changes slightly. For example, on an intraday chart you will look at the 20-*period* moving average, or the 50-*period* (rather than a 20-day or 50-day on a daily chart). I mention this because many traders don't realize this. In other words, a 50-period or 200-period moving average refers to an intraday chart. Intraday charts, however, have time frames such as a 5-minute, 15-minute, or 60-minute. Therefore, on a 5-minute chart, each candlestick, bar, or period represents 5 minutes. On a 60-minute chart, each candlestick, bar, or period represents 60 minutes. Another tidbit: a 10-period moving average on a 10-minute chart uses a total of 100 minutes of price action to calculate the moving average.

All day traders have their favorite time frames, but on a 60-minute chart, the 65-period and 135-period are popular.

USING EXPONENTIAL MOVING AVERAGES

For more precise information, consider using exponential moving averages, which are calculated the same as simple moving averages, but give more weight to the most recent time periods.

Moving average experts point out that the simple moving average, although useful, can be a little slow to respond to market changes. So if given a choice between the simple and exponential, many traders choose the exponential.

In the chart shown in **Figure 4.1**, we'll look at the 10-, 12-, and 13-period exponential moving average of the S&P 500 on a 60-minute chart.

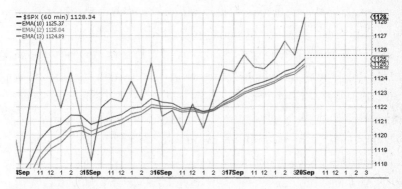

FIG 4.1: Exponential Moving Average, 60-minute   Source: Stockcharts.com

USING MOVING AVERAGES

Often, it's useful to step back and use moving averages to look at the market from a long-term perspective. Looking at the big picture, when a stock crosses the 200-day moving average in either direction, more than likely, there will be a reaction. The same is true for the 20-day MA and 50-day MA. Large numbers of traders watch these major moving averages, and it's something that you can do. As you see more and more of the crossovers, you can record the data in your trade journal, and eventually you may have enough information to decide if these crossings represent a tradable signal for you.

THE MOVING AVERAGE CROSSOVER STRATEGY

As a day trader, however, your big picture will be much shorter. For example, if the stock price crosses below the 5-period, 10-period, or 20-period moving average on an intraday chart, this is a negative signal. After all, moving averages act as support and resistance, so a crossing above or below the moving average is a signal you shouldn't ignore. Other traders use the 30-period or 200-period on an intraday chart, such as on a 30-minute or 60-minute chart.

A popular longer-term signal: if the 8-day moving average (the shorter moving average) crosses *above* the 13-day moving average (the longer moving average), this could be a buy signal. Conversely, if the 8-day moving average crosses *below* the 13-day moving average, this could be a sell signal. Once again, day traders use intraday charts such as the 60-minute, 15-minute, and 5-minute for signals rather than the daily chart.

Although moving averages are useful, they aren't perfect. First of all, they're called *lagging* indicators because they sometimes give late signals. By the time you notice the signal, the setup has passed. Also, moving averages work well when a stock is trending, but if the stock is in a *trading range* (choppy and trendless), moving averages don't seem to work as well. Even with these limitations, moving averages are signals you shouldn't ignore, and most day traders study them closely.

Taking Moving Averages to a Higher Level: MACD

The Moving Average Convergence Divergence (MACD), a technical indicator popular with many traders, also helps to identify when trends may be beginning or ending. Created by Gerald Appel in 1976, MACD consists of two lines, a solid black line called the MACD line, and a dotted red (or gray) line called the 9-day signal line, which is actually a moving average of a moving average.

The MACD line is the faster of the two lines (the shorter the time period, the faster the line). The key to understanding MACD is observing how the faster MACD line interacts with the slower signal line. (In case you are interested, MACD is the difference between the 12- and 26-day exponential moving averages. The signal line is the exponential moving average of MACD).

MACD generates a number of signals that traders look for. For example, when MACD crosses above the 9-day signal line, this may be a buy signal. And if MACD crosses below the 9-day signal line, this may be a sell signal.

In addition, you will also see a flat, horizontal centerline, the "zero" line. If MACD crosses above the zero line, this could be a buy signal. Conversely, if MACD crosses below the zero line, this could be a sell signal.

If you've never used technical indicators before, you might wonder how they work. The answer lies in the formula, which can get complicated. MACD, as mentioned earlier, is a calculation of the difference between the closing prices of two exponential moving averages. The result is displayed on a chart alongside a moving average of the difference.

Figure 4.2 is what MACD looks like on a daily chart.

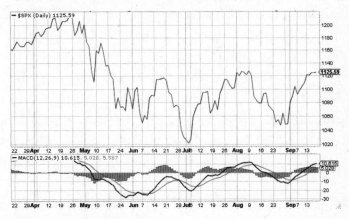

FIG 4.2: MACD   Source: Stockcharts.com

Because MACD is such a flexible indicator, you have a choice of settings. Although the default settings are 12, 26, and 9 (12-day exponential moving average, 26-day exponential moving average, and 9-day signal line), as a day trader, you'll use much shorter signals. Nevertheless, you might also want to view MACD on multiple time frames, for example, daily and weekly charts, to get a big picture view.

Consider experimenting with a setting of 6, 19, and 9, as suggested by Appel in his book, *Power Tools for Active Investors*. Appel also says that traders should pay particular attention when MACD crosses over the zero line because he believes this signal has better odds of being correct. For example, if MACD crosses over the zero line, this *may* be a buy signal. If MACD crosses below the zero line, this *could* be a sell signal. Why can't I give you a more definitive answer? First, no indicator is perfect, and there is always the chance for false signals. Second, you don't want to enter a large position based on the results of one indicator. Rather, many traders use indicators to confirm what they already see on a chart. The signal helps them make a decision.

Another signal to look for is *divergence*, for example, if price moves up but MACD moves down, and vice versa. Many traders look for signs of divergence in MACD and believe it can lead to a profitable trade.

In addition, many traders rely on the MACD histogram developed by Thomas Aspray. A histogram is plotted on top of MACD, giving a visual representation of price momentum (e.g., the rate of the speed of rising or falling stock prices). As the "peaks and valleys" of the histogram get smaller, it means that momentum is slowing down, perhaps signaling a change in direction. Conversely, as the peaks and valleys get taller and deeper, it may signal that momentum is increasing.

To fully appreciate MACD, you must take the time to experiment with the settings. If you choose to use this indicator, you'll probably use multiple time frames with a variety of settings. MACD can be used on very short-term charts (e.g., 5-minute, 15-minute, and 60-minute) to daily, weekly, or monthly.

Volatility Rules: Bollinger Bands

Bollinger Bands, created by John Bollinger in the 1980s, are popular with day traders because they're so flexible and easy to use. When you first plot Bollinger Bands on a chart, it usually appears with the default setting of a 20-period simple moving average and 2 standard deviations (20, 2). (Put another way, the default setting is the upper and lower Bollinger Bands placed at a distance of 2 standard deviations from a 20-period simple moving average.)

In the chart in Figure 4.3, you'll see four lines. The most volatile line is price. You will also see an upper, middle, and lower Bollinger Band. The middle Bollinger Band (the dotted line) is the default 20-day moving average. It is the base for the upper and lower bands and is used to describe the current trend. When you select Bollinger Bands from the list of indicators that are included in your chart program, it will be displayed on the chart, as you'll see in **Figure 4.3**. **Figure 4.3** shows Bollinger Bands on a 60-minute chart.

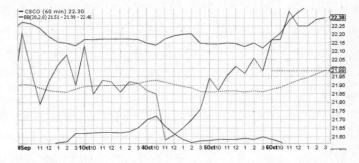

FIG 4.3: Bollinger Bands   Source: Stockcharts.com

When the stock price tags or pierces the upper band, it means the stock is *overbought* (there has been too much buying). Look at the chart above for an overbought signal. Conversely, when the stock price pierces the lower band, it means the stock is *oversold* (there has been too much selling). Keep in mind that just because a stock is overbought or oversold doesn't mean that a reversal is imminent.

In fact, stocks and indexes can remain overbought or oversold for long time periods. On the other hand, sometimes stocks will pierce the upper and lower band and immediately reverse direction, and head directly for the center.

Keep in mind that for a stock to pierce the upper or lower band, it takes a very strong move. After all, the default setting is 2 standard deviations, which is well outside the norm.

Although there are no guarantees, it's not surprising if a stock reverses direction when it pierces the upper or lower band. The best advice: when a stock is overbought or oversold based on Bollinger Bands, you should pay attention, but it isn't necessarily an actionable trade.

In addition to observing overbought and oversold conditions, day traders also look at the shape of the bands. A band that is contracting, or squeezing together, means that volatility is low. This is a clue that the stock may reverse direction. Conversely, if a band is expanding, which reflects high volatility, the stock could reverse direction.

Usually, stocks won't remain in this condition for very long. As a day trader, you use Bollinger Bands to identify extreme conditions and only take action after confirming with other indicators. Like all of the indicators included in this chapter, you have to put them on a chart and use them. That is the only way you'll learn if they work for you.

Taking a Roller Coaster Ride: Oscillators

The next two indicators, Relative Strength Indicator (RSI) and Stochastics, are called oscillators because they move up and down between 0 and 100 on a chart. Although they're created using complex formulas, they're relatively easy to use.

The hard part, of course, is correctly interpreting the indicator's signals. The main purpose of these oscillators is to determine if a stock or index such as the S&P 500 is overbought or oversold. The ideal environment for oscillators is when there is a lot of volatility. Oscillators are often most effective during these conditions. Let's take a look at how you can use the two most popular oscillators, RSI and Stochastics.

THE DRAMA KING: RSI

When you select Relative Strength Indicator (RSI) from your brokerage firm software, this momentum oscillator appears as a single line on the top or bottom of a chart. Because it has only one signal line, it's relatively easy to use. Originally created by J. Welles Wilder, RSI is often used by short-term traders to help determine whether a stock is overbought or oversold.

To be specific, when RSI rises above 70, it's a signal that a stock or market is overbought. Conversely, when RSI drops below 30, it's a signal that a stock or market is oversold. As mentioned earlier, a stock can remain overbought or oversold for lengthy time periods before reversing direction.

Keep in mind that the 30 and 70 levels are only guidelines and not fixed rules. Often, during bull markets or bear markets, the RSI levels adjust according to market conditions, so it's important to be flexible when using this indicator.

Figure 4.4 is what RSI looks like on a 60-minute chart:

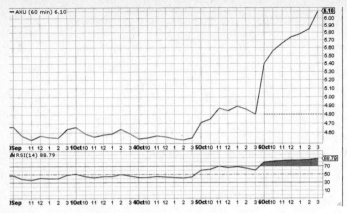

FIG 4.4: RSI   Source: Stockcharts.com

Start with the default 14-day signal for a longer-term signal, but experiment with the 9-day to see how RSI reacts. In addition, some day traders have been known to use 2-day RSI settings. The goal, of course, is to find a setting that works for you, and the only way to find out is by trying different settings. You can record the results in your journal, and eventually you'll be able to make sense of the data.

Another signal you can look for is *divergence*, which occurs when the stock is hitting new lows but RSI is rising. The idea is for the stock to follow RSI as it increases. With divergences, if the indicator is moving up, but price is moving down, you'd consider buying. Conversely, if the indicator is moving down, but price is moving up, you'd consider selling.

Although divergences are usually very effective, unfortunately, several traders have reported that RSI divergences have not been very effective. You'll have to experiment on your own to see if these traders are correct.

As with any indicator, especially oscillators using short-term time frames, false signals are possible. Only with practice, experience, and careful record keeping can you learn to trust your indicator and be confident of its signals.

THE DRAMA QUEEN: STOCHASTICS

Many day traders favor Stochastics, created by Ralph Dystant and George Lane. While RSI uses only one signal line, Stochastics uses two and sometimes three. Because RSI and Stochastics measure whether stocks are overbought or oversold (among other things), traders often use one of these indicators, but usually not both.

Since Stochastics uses multiple signal lines, it is more volatile than RSI. However, because of the way the formula is calculated, Stochastics can give more accurate and precise results. On the other hand, because of its volatility, it can sometimes give false signals, especially when using short time frames. Many experienced traders use Stochastics, but it definitely takes some time to learn.

When you select Stochastics from your charting software, you usually have three choices: Slow Stochastics, Fast Stochastics, and Full Stochastics. As a new day trader, select Slow Stochastics. The reason? It's easier to use and it generates fewer signals. As you gain more experience, you can experiment with Fast Stochastics. When first starting off, however, it's probably best to stick with the slower signal. The only downside with Slow Stochastics is it has a slight signal lag. At first, though, your goal is to learn all of the nuances of the various indicators, and Slow Stochastics is a good place to start.

Let's look at Slow Stochastics on a 60-minute chart (see **Figure 4.5**):

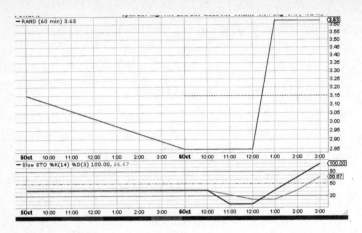

FIG 4.5: Stochastics Source: Stockcharts.com

Since we chose Slow Stochastics in the chart above, you'll notice two lines that come in two speeds. The first, %D, is the slower line, while the second line, %K, is faster. The lines are based on a mathematical formula that looks at the moving average, the highest high, and the highest low.

Some of the signals to look for: If %D rises above 80, that suggests the stock is overbought. Conversely, if %D drops below 20, that usually means the stock is oversold. In the chart above, notice the stock is well above 80, a signal it is in overbought territory.

Just as with RSI, stocks or indexes can remain overbought or oversold for long time periods before reversing direction. It's always best to confirm using other indicators to determine if the stock may reverse.

A mistake made by traders in the past was assuming that as soon as %D pierced 80, the stock should be sold. Other bad advice: As soon as %D pierced 20, the stock should be bought. These hard and fast rules were rather misleading for traders.

Nevertheless, here are a few of the most useful signals: if %D rises above 80, look for an opportunity to sell. Conversely, if %D drops below 20, look for an opportunity to buy.

Another popular signal: When %D and %K diverge. For example, if %D is moving up while the stock is moving down, it's possible the stock will follow %D. Conversely, if %D is moving down while the stock is moving up, it's possible the stock will follow. If it does follow, you may have an actionable trade. Unlike RSI, traders report that divergences in Stochastics are more reliable; that is, Stochastic divergences work more times than not. Again, be sure to enter what you've learned about Stochastics into your trading diary.

On Balance Volume (OBV)

On Balance Volume (OBV), originally developed by Joe Granville in the 1960s, is used to measure how much volume is flowing into or out of an individual security. This relatively simple indicator displays a cumulative volume total (when a stock rises for the day, volume is added; when a stock falls for the day, volume is subtracted). When displayed on a chart, OBV can graphically show whether volume is increasing or decreasing. At the most basic level, a rising OBV is a bullish signal, while a falling OBV is bearish.

Traders also compare the OBV with price to look for either divergence or confirmation. If a divergence exists, OBV is expected to move in the opposite direction. To be specific, if price is moving higher while OBV is moving lower (divergence), that is a negative signal. Many traders claim OBV's most useful signal is divergence.

Conversely, if it is confirming the price move, OBV should move in the same direction. Therefore, if price is moving higher and OBV is moving higher (confirmation), this could indicate that the upward rise in the stock is strong.

Hint: a rising OBV line means that volume is increasing on up days. Look at the stock price to see if it is moving in the same direction, which confirms the price uptrend.

Introducing More Technical Indicators

Almost all of the technical indicators introduced above can be used to monitor the overall market and/or individual stocks (except for OBV, which is used for individual stocks). The indicators I'll introduce next, however, are primarily used to monitor the broad market such as the S&P 500 or Nasdaq Composite.

As a day trader, although you will primarily focus on intraday action, it is also useful to study the direction of the overall market. The following indicators can help.

ANOTHER FAVORITE INDICATOR: NEW HIGH-NEW LOW

New High-New Low tracks the number of stocks that are making new highs and new lows, usually over a 52-week period. This straightforward indicator is quite easy to calculate and interpret. For example, when New High-New Low is positive, it means that the number of stocks making new highs exceeds the number making new lows, a bullish signal. Conversely, when New High-New Low is negative, it means new lows are surpassing new lows, a bearish signal.

Here is what New High-New Low looks like on a daily chart. On **Figure 4.6,** the Nasdaq and NYSE new highs and new lows are combined:

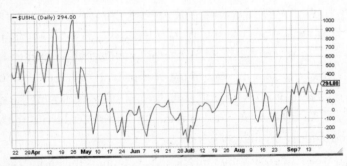

FIG 4.6: New High-New Low   Source: Stockcharts.com

The New High-New Low has been a favorite of day traders for some time. In fact, trader and psychiatrist Dr. Alexander Elder has written in his best-selling books that the New High-New Low is one of the best indicators for short-term traders.

As you look more closely at this indicator, you can see whether new highs or new lows are expanding. After all, if new highs are expanding, especially on rising volume, this is a positive sign. Conversely, if new lows are expanding on rising volume, this is a negative sign.

Traders also look for signs of divergence; that is, if the market is going higher but if the stocks on the new high list are suddenly dropping off. This could be another sign the market may reverse to the downside. And of course, if the market is going lower but stocks on the new low list are dropping off, the market may reverse to the upside.

Finally, if the list of stocks making new highs is expanding too rapidly, it could actually be a negative signal. After all, if every stock is making new highs, some might conclude there are too few stocks left to buy. It's the same with new lows. If too many stocks are making new lows, and the number reaches extreme levels, you could conclude there are too few stocks able to go lower. If only sellers remain, perhaps the market is ripe for a reversal.

Instead of the default 52-week New High-New Low, some short-term traders recommend using the 20-day New High-New Low, which they feel gives a more precise signal for short-term traders.

A DAY TRADER'S TOOL: ARMS INDEX (TRIN)

The Arms Index, also known as the TRIN, was created by Richard Arms in the 1960s. Many short-term traders use this indicator to evaluate whether the overall market is overbought or oversold.

Basically, the Arms Index calculates how much volume is associated with rising or declining stock prices on the NYSE or Nasdaq.

The results are displayed as a ratio: the lower the ratio, (i.e., below 0.50) the more bullish it is for the stock market. The lower ratio means the market is getting so overexuberant, a reversal may be imminent.

Conversely, a high ratio is bearish for the stock market, and means there is excessive selling. In this case, the market is getting so panicky that a reversal is possible. Is it definitely going to reverse direction? Unfortunately, it's extremely difficult to predict reversals, which is why it's possible, but not guaranteed. It's all about probabilities. That is another reason why traders will consult other indicators to help make a decision.

Although simple to plot on a chart, interpreting the results of the Arms Index can be a challenge. It must be studied and observed closely before using it for market timing. Day traders who have done their homework claim it's extremely useful as a timing tool, although it takes time to learn its nuances.

Figure 4.7 is the Arms Index on a daily chart:

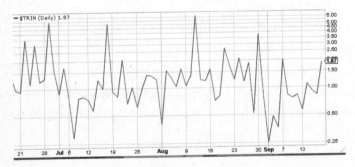

FIG 4.7: Arms Index   Source: Stockcharts.com

It's best not to make hard and fast rules about when and how to use the Arms Index. Generally, if this indicator moves above 2.0 on the market close (there is excessive selling), some traders may see this as a buy signal. If the Arms Index shoots past 4.0 or higher on the close, it indicates panic. A reversal may be imminent.

Conversely, if the Arms Index drops below 0.50 on the close (there is excessive buying), the market may reverse. Some traders will see this as a sell signal. If the Arms Index drops as low as 0.30, this means the buying has reached extreme levels. Some traders will see this as a climatic high and look for selling opportunities.

Also, a few short-term traders plot a moving average such as the 10-day MA to the Arms Index to smooth out the volatility. Be sure to consider all of these signals as guidelines rather than actionable trades.

DETERMINING MARKET BREADTH: ADVANCE-DECLINE LINE

The Advance-Decline Line is a deceptively simple indicator that tracks a running total of the difference between the number of advancing stocks and the number of declining stocks. The idea is to help traders determine market *breadth*, or how many stocks are participating in a rising or falling market.

As can be seen in the chart in **Figure 4.8**, when the Advance-Decline Line is rising, that's a bullish sign. When the Advance-Decline Line is falling, that's bearish. It can't get much easier than that!

Although financial websites and periodicals list the number of advances and declines, it's a lot easier to display the totals on a chart. You can quickly see which way the market could be headed.

Figure 4.8 is a chart of the Advance-Decline Line:

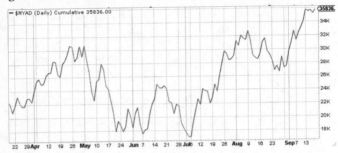

FIG 4.8: Advance-Decline Line   Source: Stockcharts.com

One way to use the Advance-Decline Line is to look for signs of divergence, that is, the market is going up but the Advance-Decline Line is falling. It could mean that the number of advancing stocks is losing steam, and could be a clue the trend is about to end. Keep in mind, however, that when the Advance-Decline Line and market are moving in the same direction, the signal is stronger.

Although the Advance-Decline Line is extremely useful to traders, there are a few nuances to using it. For example, sometimes the values mentioned earlier are lagging, which is why this indicator is not ideal for timing the market.

In addition, one of the criticisms of the NYSE Advance-Decline Line is that the NYSE, which is where this indicator gets its data, has been skewed with nonoperating issues such as closed-end bond funds. Critics say these interest-rate-sensitive issues don't provide an accurate indication of what the stock market is really doing.

Tom McClellan, whose parents Sherman and Marian originally developed the McClellan Oscillator in 1969, claims that removing nonoperating issues could be a mistake. "Throwing out the nonoperating issues seems like a good idea, but it destroys the good information that the Advance-Decline Line gives."

McClellan says that you want to watch these interest-rate-sensitive issues to measure liquidity. "These interest-rate-sensitive issues, which are really liquidity sensitive, are the real canaries in the coalmine," he says. "They are the ones that will do well when liquidity is good, and they will suffer when liquidity is getting scarce." In fact, McClellan likes to study nonoperating issues and common stocks separately.

NYSE TICK

Some day traders rely on the NYSE TICK to monitor what is occurring on the New York Stock Exchange (NYSE) issues. The calculation is rather simple: If, for example, 1,000 stocks moved up on the last trade (uptick) and 600 stocks moved down on the last trade, the TICK will display a reading of +400, a positive signal. If the TICK reads +200, it means that 200 more NYSE stocks moved up on the last trade (uptick) than moved down. Conversely, a -200 TICK reading means 200 more NYSE stocks moved down on the last trade (downtick) than moved up, a negative signal.

Sometimes the TICK shows extreme conditions, which is a clue the market may be oversold or overbought. Based on probabilities, a reversal could occur. Usually, extremes on the TICK are + 1,000 or -1,000, but they are unlikely to stay at these extreme levels for very long.

Traders use the TICK to compare the number of upticks versus downticks. When buyers are in control and more aggressive, you'll see more upticks. Conversely, if sellers are more aggressive and in control, you'll see more downticks. Tracked over time, the TICK gives interesting insights into market sentiment.

TICK statistics are published live on the web, the Nasdaq website, and your brokerage firm. Hint: place TICK statistics on your trading screen along with a handful of your favorite indicators. (It's probably too early for you to have any favorite indicators, but eventually you will).

For Experienced Traders: The McClellan Oscillator

Experienced traders often turn to the McClellan Oscillator and the McClellan Summation Index for more precise information than the Advance-Decline Line can give. This indicator receives its information from the net advances and net declines and gives traders overbought and oversold indications and divergences. It also measures the power of a move. The Oscillator measures the acceleration that takes place within the daily breadth numbers, which make up the Advance-Decline Line. (For example, if price increases by 50 points a day, you get a measure of the speed of the market. However, if it only increases by 40 points, it is decelerating. The market is still increasing, but at a slower rate.)

For day traders who want to trade with the trend and are looking for detailed information, this oscillator might be what you're looking for. Nevertheless, it's not as easy to learn as the indicators mentioned earlier. That's why I recommend you first learn everything you can about the Advance-Decline Line before tackling the McClellan Oscillator.

Here's an example of how this Oscillator works: when the 19-day exponential moving average (EMA) is below the 39-day EMA, it will generate a negative value. It means that declining issues are stronger than advancing issues. Conversely, if the 19-day EMA is above the 39-day EMA, it will generate a positive value. It means that advancing issues are stronger than declining issues.

In addition, the McClellan Oscillator also generates a number of sophisticated values that help traders determine the overall breadth of the market. Although this indicator can be somewhat intimidating at first, many traders use it in conjunction with the Advance-Decline Line.

Tom McClellan explains: "The McClellan Oscillator doesn't just tell you the position of the Advance-Decline Line on a chart, but its acceleration. It tells you how fast or slow the line is moving, upward or downward. For example, if you see a price move that is not accompanied by rapid acceleration, this could be very important information."

McClellan cautions, however, that his indicator should not be the first one you learn how to use. "You can't really understand the McClellan Oscillator without first understanding a little bit about the Advance-Decline Line statistics," he cautions. "You should know these statistics are published every day."

The McClellan Oscillator isn't a silver bullet. "It's not going to tell you something different than the Advance-Decline Line," McClellan explains. "But it will give you more in-depth information so you'll know the complete story."

Unfortunately, not everyone completely understands how to properly use this oscillator. "If all you do is look at the numerical value of the McClellan Oscillator," McClellan says, "you're ignoring 99 percent of the most useful information. If all you know is the number, you don't know what the trend is. It's like forecasting the weather by only knowing the current temperature. That would be a very limited way of forecasting. Therefore, you can only use the McClellan Oscillator if you understand its value relative to yesterday or last week." The key to understanding the oscillator, he says, is looking at it on a chart. After all, a picture is worth a thousand words.

Chapter 5:
Making Your First Day Trade

I've always said that the opening of the stock market is similar to the thrilling start of the Running of the Bulls in Pamplona, Spain. This is when the bulls are let loose to run in a narrow street on the way to the stadium. And just like those souls who boldly run in front of the bulls, some unsuspecting traders enter The Street without fully appreciating they're in an unpredictable and dangerous environment, and end up getting gored by the herd.

Remember, like any occupation, day trading takes skill, knowledge, and dedication. If you enter the market without the proper tools or education, you could be in for an unwelcome surprise.

To be on the safe side, take as much time as needed to study the stock market and day trading strategies. If you joined a professional trading firm, they probably wouldn't let you trade for an entire year. That's right: they would make you train for a year before committing real money to the market. Keep that in mind as you read through this chapter.

Note: you can, however, get started immediately with paper trading using your brokerage firm software. Only you can decide when you're ready to trade with real money.

Let's Get Started!

Although you shouldn't be in a rush to start trading, it's time for us to move from theory into practice. Along the way, continue writing down your experiences in your trading journal. Many professional traders say that one of the most helpful exercises, and a key to their success, is keeping detailed records of lessons learned.

Taking it one step at a time, let's learn how to buy and sell stocks. If you've bought stocks before, the information in this chapter will seem familiar, although day trading is an entirely different ballgame.

Create a Trading Plan

Almost every professional trader creates a well-thought-out trading plan before the market opens, either the night before or early in the morning. They often begin by scanning for stocks that fit their criteria.

Many trading ideas can be found by looking at a stock chart. Some traders use scanning software (provided by your brokerage firm or a third-party source) to help pick stocks. By the time you finish the book, however, you'll know where to get stock ideas. If you're still unsure, I provide numerous resources in the last chapter.

It's a personal choice whether to use software or to look at charts manually. At first, do it the old fashioned way: manually. After you've gained more experience and have a better understanding of what to look for, you'll probably be grateful that software is available.

> When looking for stocks to buy, avoid the
> cheap or illiquid stocks. It's better to buy and
> sell higher-quality stocks, even if they are
> more expensive.

Hint: although some traders combine technical and fundamental analysis when looking for stocks to buy, day traders rely primarily on technical analysis to decide when to enter or exit.

For each stock that meets your criteria, you'll need to write down on paper:

1. Your expected purchase price.
2. A realistic selling price using technical analysis.
3. An exit price in case you were wrong about the stock. This can be your stop-loss, that is, the price that you will exit a stock. Knowing this price in advance can help prevent you from losing even more money.

Writing these three prices on paper is a key ingredient of your trading plan. In the heat of battle, when emotions can run high, you will focus on these prices.

By now, perhaps you're thinking: how do I find stocks that meet my criteria, and how do I calculate entries and exits? The answer to both questions can be found by using technical analysis. For example, stocks that are about to breakout is one possible criterion. As you continue reading, you will find many others. Also, determining proper entries and exits takes experience, and again, you'll use technical analysis (support and resistance, for example) for guidance. One guideline: get out of a stock quickly if doesn't do what you expected. (I'll have more to say about stop-losses later.)

THE RISK-REWARD CALCULATION

Next, you need to determine a *risk-reward ratio*. In other words, before you enter a stock, you want to make sure that buying and selling it will be worth the effort. Put another way, you enter the trade if the monetary reward is high enough to justify the trade and the risk relatively low. The pros call this a favorable risk-reward, which is usually expressed as a ratio. Determining a favorable risk-reward is one of the key ingredients to proper money management.

The risk-reward ratio can be either simple or complicated to calculate. I've read articles on calculating the risk-reward ratio that you'd need an advanced degree in mathematics to understand. Based on my personal experience, the more complicated the calculation, the less likely anyone will follow it. Therefore, I'm going to introduce the most basic risk-reward ratio.

The biggest problem with calculating the risk-reward ratio is you have to make assumptions about how much profit you "expect" to make. Although your expectation is based on technical analysis such as support and resistance, you may not be right. Therefore, risk-reward calculations have to be flexible, depending on changing market conditions.

Pros will tell you they want a risk-reward ratio of at least 1:2, and that 1:3 is even better. This means that for every $1 you risk, you "expect" to receive at least $2 or $3 in profit, or reward. (As a day trader, however, this may not always be realistic. Sometimes you have to take what you can get.)

Here's the simplest example:

You enter the stock at $20. Your stop-loss is at $19 (meaning you'll sell the stock at this price if it declines instead of advancing), so you won't lose more than 1 point on the trade (in trading, 1 point always equals $1). Based on your analysis, you plan to exit at $22 for a 2-point profit. In other words, you are risking 1 point if you are wrong, but you aim to make 2 points if right. That's a 1:2

risk-reward ratio. To make this work, you have to be realistic about your price targets; hope doesn't count.

The most important lesson from this is that you don't enter a trade unless you have a reasonably good idea you'll be profitable. If for any reason the risks are too great and the reward is too small, don't make the trade. There are thousands of other stocks you can buy.

To do an accurate risk-reward analysis, you must consider your position size. If you have too large a position in one stock, you could be putting your entire portfolio at great risk, no matter how attractive the risk-reward looks like on paper.

HOW TO CALCULATE PROFIT

Your profit is determined by the number of shares you own and how many points (remember we use the word points rather than dollars) your stock goes up or down. For example, if you have 100 shares of a stock and it moves higher by one point, you have an unrealized gain of $100. If the stock moves 3 points higher, you have an unrealized gain of $300. To turn an unrealized gain into a realized (and taxable) gain, you must sell.

Keep in mind that this also works in reverse. If you have 100 shares of a stock and it falls by 1 point, you have an unrealized loss of $100. And if your stock falls by 2 points, you have an unrealized loss of $200.

Question: if you have 1,000 shares of a stock and it rises by 2 points, how much did you make (if you sold, that is)?

Answer: $2,000 (1,000 shares x 2 points) less commissions.

THE BEST ADVICE YOU'LL EVER RECEIVE

The following advice is so important it will be repeated in another chapter: before you buy a stock, the most important calculation you can make is determining what to do if you're wrong. Although it's a lot more fun to think of how much money you "could" make, knowing in advance how much you could potentially lose will help prevent you from blowing up your account. Always think of worst-case scenarios.

The pros have a name for losses: *drawdown*, a fancy way of saying how much money you can lose in your entire account at its worst level. The pros plan for drawdown and expect it, and you should do the same. Unfortunately, the size of that drawdown can never be known in advance. Put another way, don't enter a trade with sugarplums dancing in your head while the big bad wolf is hiding in the bushes ready to pounce.

Understanding the Bid, Ask, and Spread

Three key terms for traders and investors to know are: bid, ask, and spread. Bid is the slightly lower price on the left side of the quote. It's the best currently published price at which you can sell a stock (or asset). When selling, you may accept the bid price (or try to get a higher price). The ask price is the slightly higher price on the right side of the quote. It's the best currently published price at which you can buy a stock (or asset). Put another way, it's the lowest price a seller is willing to accept for an individual security. When buying, you will pay the ask price (or occasionally less). The spread is the difference between the bid and ask prices (and in case you're wondering, the difference is pocketed by the specialists or market makers who maintain the market).

Figure 5.1 is a screen shot of Microsoft's bid, ask, and spread.

Symbol	Last	Chg.	Bid	Ask	Action	Qty	Ord.	Stop	Limit
MSFT	23.96	-0.33	23.96	24.09					
SPY	109....	-1.25	0.00	0.00	Buy ▾	⬍	▾	⬍	⬍

FIG 5.1: Bid, Ask, and Spread   For illustrative purposes only. Source: Fidelity Investments.

Put another way, the spread is the difference between what someone is willing to pay and the price at which someone is willing to sell. You'll notice that the spread is constantly in motion.

The specialists at the NYSE and the market makers on the Nasdaq usually determine the spread. They publicly display the current bid and ask price. (The only exception is if you trade via an ECN, the traders themselves determine the spread).

In the example above, the ask price for Microsoft (Nasdaq: MSFT) is $24.09. To be certain of buying Microsoft at the current market price, you'd have to pay $24.09 (or you can offer less). If you already owned Microsoft and wanted to sell it, you could sell it for the bid price of $23.96 (or you can demand more). And finally, in this example, the spread, or the difference between the bid and ask price, is $0.13.

Note: I am using Microsoft as my example because it is such a well-known company. As a day trade, however, this company is usually not volatile enough to make substantial short-term profits. The types of stocks you'll want to day trade include some of the following, the kind that can move 2, 4, or 5 percent intraday. For example: Anadarko Petroleum Corporation (NYSE: APC), American International Group (NYSE: AIG), Take-Two Interactive Software (Nasdaq: TTWO), and Blue Coat Systems (Nasdaq: BCSI). You'll find volatile stocks on the most active lists at Yahoo! Finance, Google Finance, Bloomberg, to name a few, or listed on your brokerage firm's website.

Many years ago, before stock prices were displayed as decimals, the spread could be very wide. In those days, stocks were displayed as fractions, so stocks routinely had spreads of $0.50 or more. After decimalization, which was the move from fractions to decimals, spreads of liquid, highly active stocks tightened, often to just a few pennies. One guideline: the more liquid the stock, the tighter the spread.

In fact, if you notice a very wide spread between the bid and ask, that is a warning that the stock is likely to be illiquid. Illiquid stocks are usually difficult to buy or sell. More than likely, if you see a wide spread, you're either in the after-hours market or you're looking at a penny stock trading for under $3. As a day trader, you need liquid stocks, which is why you want to avoid most penny stocks and the after-hours market.

Trading Long, Trading Short

Professional day traders know every market has two sides, long and short. Although it's challenging enough to trade on the long side, as an emerging day trader, you should also learn how to short.

When you invest in a stock hoping that it will rise in price, you are said to be *long* the stock. Your goal is to buy low and sell high. Your profit is the difference between the price at which you bought the stock and your selling price. For example, if you buy a stock at $15.23 and sell it at $16.80, you made a profit of 1.57 points.

On the other hand, if you sell stock and hope that it will go down in price, you are said to be *short* the stock. When you short a stock, you first sell the stock, hoping to buy it back at a lower price. Your profit is the difference between the price at which you sold the stock and the price at which you bought it back. If you've never shorted stocks before, it can seem a bit counterintuitive. But once you learn how to use this strategy, you'll gladly pull it out during certain market conditions.

SHORTING BASICS

Here's how shorting works: let's say you're watching the stock Daytraders, Inc. and, based on the signals listed below, you believe this $50 stock is overbought and ready for a fall. If you decide to sell short 100 shares of Daytraders, Inc., you place an order to sell Daytraders, Inc. at $50 per share.

Because you don't own the stock, the brokerage firm lends you 100 shares of Daytraders, Inc. You sell the shares, collect $5,000 (100 shares x $50 per share), and your trade confirmation shows that you sold the shares and that your current position in the stock is minus (-) 100 shares. If your analysis is correct, Daytraders, Inc. eventually falls to $49. You then turn around and buy 100 shares for $4,900, thereby covering the short position. You now have a 1-point profit, or $100. The shares you bought (+100 shares) cancel the prior position (-100 shares) and you no longer have a position. The brokerage firm takes the shares you just bought and returns them to the lender. You have the $100 profit (less commissions).

Many pros say they can make more money on the short side. The reason? Shorting opportunities often occur with a huge, volatile move down, which means the potential for large profits. When people buy, they tend to do it more gradually (unless it's in the later stages of a buying climax), but when people sell, especially when afraid, they tend to do it in one huge move.

The ideal time to short is in a downtrend. You also want to find stocks that are below their moving average and are the lagging stocks in a sector or industry group.

WHAT CAN GO WRONG

Although selling short sounds straightforward, a lot of things can go wrong. When you go long a stock, in theory you could lose everything you invested. But when you short a stock, you could lose more than you invested, which is why shorting can be risky.

For example, what if Daytraders, Inc. didn't drop by 1 point but increased in value? In that case, for every point that Daytraders, Inc. rises, you lose $100. How high can a stock go up? It's unlimited. The problem with shorting is if a stock goes up, not down, your losses are unlimited, if you don't cover or use stops.

CONTROLLING RISK

Shorting has a bad reputation among uninformed (and undisciplined) investors who don't understand its nuances. When shorting, you should have tight stops and the discipline to cover your position if it's going against you. In addition, when you have a substantial profit from a short, use trailing stops to protect your profit. Investors don't remain panicked forever, so stocks will eventually reverse and head higher. Then again, it's difficult to predict when this might occur.

Although experienced short sellers are disciplined enough to cover their shorts quickly before the position gets out of control, mistakes can and do occur. For example, as a day trader, you probably don't want to hold any losing position overnight. That includes short positions. Just like with long positions, you must closely monitor your position.

> As a rookie day trader, you'll have your hands full trying to understand the long side of the market. That is why I recommend that you first understand the long side before shorting. Although selling short can be profitable, at times this strategy can be extremely challenging.

If You've Never Bought or Sold a Stock: Read This

If you're familiar with buying and selling stocks, feel free to skip this short section. If, however, you've never bought or sold a stock, you're in the right place.

You've scanned for stocks that fit your criteria (again, this will be based on technical analysis or scanning software from your brokerage firm) and you decide to buy 100 shares of Microsoft Corporation (Nasdaq: MSFT), which is trading for $23.96 per share (but it's guaranteed to change by the time you read this).

To get started, sign onto your brokerage firm's website. After logging in, you will enter the trading area of your firm's website. Your screen could look similar to what is displayed in **Figure 5.2**.

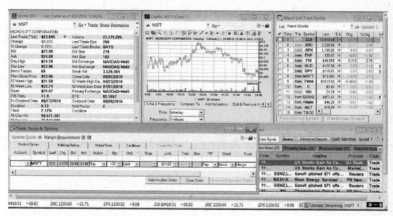

FIG 5.2: Main Screen, Brokerage Website   For illustrative purposes only. Source: Fidelity Investments. © 2010 FMR LLC. All rights reserved. Used by permission.

UNDERSTANDING THE MAIN SCREEN

In the main screen (**Figure 5.2**), moving from left to right, you'll see a detailed quote of Microsoft with important information such as the day's high and low, and the bid and ask price. Next, an intraday candlestick chart of Microsoft is displayed.

Notice at the bottom of the chart that you can add or change indicators, time, and frequency. The third screen is a watch list of individual stocks. On the bottom left is an order entry screen. This is the screen where you'll place your trades.

To the right is the breaking news feed, which you will observe. (Please don't make the common mistake of buying shares of a stock after you read about it in a breaking news story). And finally, on the bottom of the screen is a streaming quote.

CUSTOMIZING YOUR SCREENS

With any brokerage firm software that you use, you will have the flexibility to customize the screens to meet your needs. On any main screen, you can change the layout and colors, set up alerts, create customizable charts, generate reports, and trade stocks or options. As you gain more experience trading, you'll learn to customize your screens so that they display only the most important information. For example, you'll want to see charts with multiple time frames, technical indicators, news feeds, profit and loss results, and, of course, an order entry screen. If you have more than one monitor, you'll have a lot more real estate for other useful screens.

There are hundreds of choices you can choose from, so what you do or don't include is a personal choice. At first, all of this information may seem overwhelming, but don't worry, it will eventually get easier.

Order Types

In order to place the right order, you need to understand the difference between various order types, including market orders, limit orders, and buy-stop orders.

FAST BUT NOT RECOMMENDED: MARKET ORDER

A market order is simply telling your broker to buy the shares at the best available price. If you choose to buy or sell using market orders, then you're letting the market, which is really automated computers, fill your order using the national best bid and offer price (NBBO). This means that your broker must guarantee that you receive the best available bid and ask price.

Unfortunately, during certain market conditions, such as a fast market, if you use a market order, you may receive a very bad fill. In fact, one of the only reasons you'd select a market order is if you must have an immediate fill, but even then you may not get the most competitive price.

A market order can be a disaster. For example, during a very fast market, or *flash crash*, your sell order may be filled 10, 15, or 20 points lower than you anticipated. Although a flash crash is a relatively rare event, remember that, when you place a market order, you're giving the market full control of your order, and that's never the wisest move.

Buy Example: Microsoft is trading at $23.82 (bid) by $23.83 (ask). You enter a market order to buy, and within seconds, your order is filled at $23.83.

Sell Example: Microsoft is trading at $23.82 by $23.83. You enter a market order to sell, and seconds later, your order is filled at $23.82.

Another problem with market orders is *slippage* (the difference between the estimated market price and the actual price you bought or sold). On occasion, slippage is expected, which can cut into your profits. Because of all of the reasons mentioned above, day traders will rarely use market orders, and instead use limit orders.

COMPETITIVE AND TIMELY: LIMIT ORDER

When you enter a limit order, you decide the maximum price you are willing to pay or the minimum price you are willing to sell. Your order is filled when the stock reaches the price you specify. When buying, your limit order is at a price lower than the current ask price. When selling, your limit order is at a price higher than the current bid price. Basically, you're instructing the brokerage firm to buy at or better than the specified price. You set the parameters. Know this: the stock may be trading near $23, but if you want to bid $22.50, you may do so. There is little chance the order will be filled immediately, but you are allowed to enter a limit order at any price.

Although limit orders are the preferred method of buying or selling stock, they have a downside. For example, if the stock never reaches the limit price, your order won't be filled at all. You'll be left dangling with nowhere to go unless you re-enter your price.

Buy Example: Microsoft is trading with an ask price of $23.83, which is the price you must pay if you want to buy it right now. You set a limit order at $23.50, which guarantees that you won't pay more than $23.50 to buy this stock. If Microsoft drops to $23.50 or less, the order will be filled. If, however, the stock never drops to $23.50, the order is not triggered, you did not buy the shares, and there is no harm done.

Sell Example: Microsoft is trading at a bid price of $23.82, which is the price you'll receive if you want to sell it right now. You set a limit order to sell at $24. If Microsoft rises to $24 or above, your order is filled. If the stock does not reach $24, the order isn't filled.

If you want to get filled immediately, you may enter an order that is higher than the current ask price or lower than the bid price. In other words, if the current ask on the stock is $23.83 per share, and you want to buy immediately, you can enter $23.84. More than likely, you'll be filled immediately, and probably at $23.83.

Conversely, if the current bid price is $23.82, and you want to sell immediately, you can enter a price of $23.81. You'll probably be filled within one second.

GOING HIGHER: BUY-STOP ORDER

Another convenient type of order is the *buy-stop*. Let's say you don't want to miss out if a stock suddenly moves higher (based on a bullish chart pattern, for example). By entering a buy-stop, you're telling the brokerage firm to enter an order to buy the stock at a higher price. As soon as that price is reached, your order becomes a market order to buy.

Example of a buy-stop order: Microsoft is currently trading at $23.82 by $23.83. You enter a buy-stop order at $24. If the stock hits $24, it turns into a market order. Once the order is triggered at the buy-stop price of $24 (or higher), it will be filled at the next available price. On the other hand, if the stock doesn't hit $24 (or higher), the order will remain unfilled.

You can also use this order if you want to buy a stock at a higher price, but are away from your computer and can't enter it manually. Perhaps you have to leave the house and don't want to miss out if the stock keeps going up. Then you could enter a buy-stop order.

The only danger with this order is if the stock suddenly gaps up, for example, at the market open. You could get filled at a much higher price than you expected. Therefore, use the buy-stop order when you must make the trade, and avoid using this order type at the market open. Another solution, however, is using a buy-stop limit order.

Example of a buy-stop limit order: Microsoft is currently trading at $23.82 by $23.83. You enter a buy-stop limit order at $24. If Microsoft does hit $24, it turns into a limit order, and the shares will be bought at $24 or better. If the stock doesn't drop below $24 after the trigger (the stop price), your order will remain open. Also, in fast markets, it's possible the market will blast through your buy order without filling. Bottom line: because these orders are so flexible, it's suggested that you first experiment with them to determine which one fulfills your needs.

Note: You also have the option of entering two prices with the buy-stop limit order. The first is the stop price, which is the trigger. The second is the limit price, that is, the most you are willing to pay for the stock. Check with your brokerage firm to learn their exact rules.

Placing Your First Order

Figure 5.3 is an order entry screen for Microsoft:

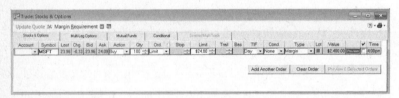

FIG 5.3: Order Entry Screen   For illustrative purposes only. Source: Fidelity Investments. © 2010 FMR LLC. All rights reserved. Used by permission.

This is an extremely important screen, one that you'll have to fully understand if you're going to trade stocks. Although the screen is easy to fill out, you need to know what each column means.

Beginning on the left, you have to enter the correct stock symbol. You wouldn't believe how many traders enter the wrong symbol and buy the wrong stock! Fortunately, there's always a preview button (on the far right) that allows you to catch mistakes before you submit the order.

The next columns are the bid-ask spread, which you just learned about. It's important that you always know the bid and ask price, and learn how to seek out the best price.

Under the Action column, you choose whether you want to buy or sell. Because we're going to buy Microsoft, we select Buy.

In the Quantity column, you select how many shares you want to buy. For this order, we enter 100 shares.

Finally, in the column Order, you have a choice of orders, limit or market. Obviously, we selected Limit.

> Anytime you're entering financial information, be sure to double-check your entries. As mentioned earlier, too many traders lose money by inadvertently entering incorrect symbols, shares, or prices. Please don't make that mistake.

Using this screen (**Figure 5.3**), we bought 100 shares of Microsoft at $24 per share. Rather than paying the current ask price of $24.09, we entered a limit price of $24. Our order may not be accepted at this price, but it's less expensive than paying the market price. As you notice on the right, the total cost of this order will be $2,400, plus commissions.

Once you've entered all the information, click on the Preview button. This gives you a chance to review your order for errors. After you press the Enter key, the order is active and ready to be filled. Good work! You've placed your first order. (By the way, our order did get filled at $24).

Once you place your first trade, you may get the same feeling you get when you skydive or drive a car for the first time. I hope that with time and experience that feeling will disappear. Why? If you're day trading because you're looking for entertainment or excitement, you'll probably end up losing money, and maybe a lot of money. Although day trading may seem like gambling to some people, if taken seriously and with the proper skills, it is an acceptable method for generating income. The goal is to trade based on probabilities and financial opportunities, not on luck or hunches.

For some people, placing an order is the easiest part of trading. Coming up next: the hard part, which is how to manage your position. Managing positions, which translates into managing risk, is what separates the pros from the amateurs.

Managing Your Position

Managing position size is one of the keys to your success as a trader, and an essential aspect of risk management. This means adjusting the size of your share position so that you aren't risking too much money in case you are wrong. For example, some rookies always buy 1,000 shares no matter what the stock price or how money they have in their account. This is a huge mistake. Proper share size is dependent on many factors, including stop-losses, which we'll discuss next.

PLAYING DEFENSE: STOCK PROTECTION ORDERS

The following types of orders are designed to lock in gains or to protect you against losses. Some traders enter these orders immediately, while others take a wait-and-see approach.

The Stop-Loss Order, Part 1: Protecting Against Large Losses

One of the more popular defensive tools is the stop-loss order, designed to protect you in case your stock starts to plunge. You use it to automatically sell a position at a specified price. Some traders enter a stop-loss as soon as they finish buying a stock, which makes sense for rookies.

The stop-loss order works like this: you buy 100 shares of Microsoft at $23.05. Next, enter a stop-loss order at $22.25, for example. Simply put, if Microsoft drops to $22.25 or less, a market order to sell 100 shares of Microsoft at "the market" is triggered. The idea is to limit losses, preventing a catastrophe.

The biggest disadvantage of the stop-loss order is there are no guarantees it will be filled at the price you want, or even executed immediately. Once it is a market order, it will be filled at the best available price.

In a normal market, the stop-loss usually works as designed, and you'll end up selling at or near $22.25 per share, in this example. An $0.80 loss is not pleasant, but it's better than losing a larger amount. You have basically contained your loss to less than a point. You can always set the stop-loss higher, for example, at $22.37, $22.70, or any other price.

Unfortunately, in a fast market where the stock gaps down, or if the market plunges, the stop-loss may not work as designed. For example, let's say the market goes into a nosedive and, on the way down, your $22.25 stop-loss is triggered. Now your market order is at the mercy of how many shares are being dumped, and how rapidly those share orders hit the trading floor (before your order). This means that it will get filled at the next available price which, in this example, could be a dozen points lower than your stop-loss price. Volatile, high-priced stocks like Google (Nasdaq: GOOG) and Apple (Nasdaq: AAPL) could gap down 5 to 15 percent (while a stodgy stock like Microsoft might only fall a little).

> If you do use a hard stop-loss (a real order that was entered through your broker), don't carry it overnight because of the possibility of market opening gap-downs (or gap-ups if you are shorting).

Determining where to enter your stop-loss is not an easy decision, but when you have determined your risk-reward, you will have a maximum loss in mind. Use that maximum loss to establish the stop-loss price. There's no right answer. Many traders use support and resistance to determine where to put a stop-loss. Other pros, however, use arbitrary percentages (1 or 2 percent) or numerical values (1 or 2 points) to determine where to put their stops. If your stops are constantly getting triggered, however, and the stock then zooms up, it's a clue you're setting your stops too tight.

The Stop-Loss Order, Part 2: Locking in Profits

Another way to use stop-loss orders is this: instead of entering in a stop-loss immediately after buying the stock, enter the stop-loss after you have an unrealized profit. In this scenario, the stop-loss is used to protect some, or all, of that profit. If the stop-loss is set above your entry price, then you will eventually realize a profit from the trade because you either sell at your target price or at the stop-loss price.

Example: You bought Microsoft at $23 per share, and it's now trading at $25 per share, a 2-point gain. You don't want to lose out on these profits so you enter a stop-loss at $24, essentially locking in a 1-point profit. If the stock continues higher, raise the stop-loss price in increments, perhaps $0.50 at a time, locking in even more profit. Keep in mind that during a hectic trading day, you may not have many opportunities to keep changing stop-loss prices. Also, always cancel any previous stop-loss orders when you replace them.

Some experienced traders take a "wait-and-see" approach and don't use hard stop-losses. Rather, they use *mental* stops. This takes more discipline, but it means that instead of actually entering the order into the computer, you either write it on paper or keep your target prices locked in your mind.

If you're a novice trader, it's best to begin by physically entering hard stops. As you gain experience and discipline, you can decide which type of order suits your trading style. The downside to using mental stops is you must watch your stock positions very closely. Unfortunately, many people lack the discipline to sell based on mental stops.

No matter which technique you use, keep this in mind: "If you are ahead by three points," says trader and bestselling author Dr. Alexander Elder, "you are not going to give back more than two. You have to protect at least one point of profit. It's absolutely criminal to take a large open profit and allow the market to turn it into a loss."

Understanding the stop-loss is an essential part of your education. That being said, instead of entering a market order, many traders use a stop-limit order, which we'll discuss next. As you'll see, each order type has advantages and disadvantages.

The Stop-Limit Order: Another Way to Protect Against Losses

The stop-limit order combines both a stop-loss and a limit order into one. Instead of entering one number, you enter two. The first number triggers the stop and the second number specifies the minimum selling price you will accept. Sounds confusing? It's not. After you try it a few times, it's easy to understand.

It works like this: let's say you bought Microsoft at $22.90 per share. When you enter a stop sell limit order, you first enter the *stop* price, for example, $22 per share. At the same time, you enter a *limit* price, which sets a limit on the lowest price you will accept for your shares. The limit price guarantees that the stock will be sold at or above that price (assuming it's sold—limit orders are sometimes not filled). In our example, we'll set a limit price of $21.95 per share.

After setting up the stop-limit order (with a $22 stop and $21.95 limit), here's what could happen in real life: Microsoft is trading at

$24 per share and it appears as if you'll be able to book a profit. Suddenly, some bad news hits the entire technology sector and Microsoft suddenly drops well below $22.90 per share.

In this example, the stop-loss order is triggered at $22 per share. Now the order becomes a limit order. Next, as long as the order can be sold at $21.95 or higher per share, the order will be filled. If however, the stock gaps down below the $21.95 limit price, the order will not be filled.

Theoretically, the stock could drop to $15 per share and your order still will not be filled, not until it rises above $21.95 per share. (By the way, if it drops to $15 a share, you'll want to cancel your sell order and devise a new trading plan.) Put another way, you are controlling exactly at what price you will sell the stock. In this example, you are telling the market you will only sell above $21.95 per share.

You could also place a $22 stop price and a $22 limit order, so that at $22 the order is triggered, but the stock must still be trading at $22 or it won't get filled. As with any order, you are telling the computer that handles the trades that you insist on receiving this price and not a penny less. In a fast-moving market, however, the chances of not getting filled increase.

To summarize, with the stop-loss market order, you will get filled, but you don't know the exact price. With a stop-limit order, you are guaranteed a certain price, but the order may not get filled if that price isn't available.

A Clever Way to Lock In Profits: Trailing Stop Orders

The trailing stop order, entered as a dollar or a percentage amount, is a more sophisticated way of locking in gains and minimizing losses. The trailing stop adjusts or trails behind a rising stock price. It's ideal for traders who don't want to enter new (and cancel older) orders.

It works like this: you buy a stock at $20 and enter a trailing stop order of $1. Every penny that the stock moves higher, the trailing stop increases by one penny. If the stock moves to $21, for example, the trailing stop order tags along, adjusting higher. In this case, if the stock falls to $20, an order is triggered, and becomes a market (or limit) order to sell. Instead of a dollar amount, you also can set a percentage, such as 1 or 2 percent.

The trailing stop order only adjusts higher, allowing you to lock in gains, but doesn't change if the stock moves lower, so it also minimizes losses.

Although the trailing stop order locks in your gains quite effectively when the gains are large, it doesn't do much if you're trading for small profits. Also, it's possible the trailing stop order might trigger too fast with very volatile stocks.

Again, it's best to experiment with the trailing stop in a practice account. These practice sessions are well worth your time. Best advice: learn how these orders work *before* you place your first trade.

Note that it's also possible to enter a trailing stop-*limit* order, which can give you even more control over your order. The trailing stop market order will definitely get you out of the stock, while the trailing stop-limit order may not get filled at all.

A SHARP ALTERNATIVE: PRICE ALERTS

If you're concerned that stop-loss orders are too permanent and that mental stops are too loose, try this flexible alternative: the price alert. Many pros successfully use price alerts to manage their orders.

It's quite simple: you instruct your brokerage firm to notify you by e-mail, phone, or with a computer beep when a specific price target has been reached for a specific stock. Therefore, even before you buy a stock, you can set up automatic price alerts for entries and exits. Alerts will tell you when your target prices for buying or selling have been reached.

For example, if you're interested in a particular stock but feel it's overpriced, you can set up a price alert for a more reasonable price.

Many disciplined traders will find alerts an excellent alternative to placing hard stops.

FOR SOPHISTICATED TRADERS: CONDITIONAL ORDERS

To gain even more control over your orders, you might want to consider using conditional orders. These instructions can be as simple or as complicated as you want.

For example, with a conditional order you can simultaneously place two orders on the same stock. For example, if your stock is trading at $20, you can place a *One Cancels the Other* (OCO) order which consists of *both* a stop-loss to sell at $19, and a limit order to sell at $22. Whichever order is triggered first is the one that is executed and the other is cancelled. This type of order is ideal for some traders because it forces them to have a trading plan with specific price targets.

You can place all kinds of conditional orders. For example, one of my acquaintances places a conditional time order. He sets up a conditional order so that his orders aren't triggered until the market is open at least 10 minutes. This way, he misses out on dangerous gap ups in the morning. As you gain more experience with conditional orders, you may also come up with new and creative combinations. (Not every brokerage firm accepts every type of conditional order, so be certain to ask first).

OTHER ORDER CHOICES

You have other choices when placing an order. For example, on the dropdown menu on your order entry screen, you may see *Good 'Til Canceled* (GTC). Because some brokers will only hold an open order until the end of the day, this order instructs your brokerage firm to keep the order active until you cancel it. As a day trader, however, it's unlikely you'll use a GTC very often, if ever.

You can also choose *All or None* (AON) which means you want the entire order filled or none at all. This prevents an order from being partially filled, 100 shares here, or 100 shares there. This is perhaps most useful for thinly traded stocks, when you either want the entire order completed, or to forget about the whole trade. Most traders tend to keep this box unchecked, and are willing to accept partial fills.

Have a Selling Strategy

Remember the following: have a selling strategy. Many rookie traders, and some experienced ones, too, spend most of their time thinking of stocks to buy but spend little time on when to sell. Because some traders don't have a selling plan and play it by ear, they lose money.

A popular Wall Street saying is: "Cut your losses short and let your winners run." As a day trader, however, you don't have the luxury of letting your winners run for too long. Once your profit goals are met, you want to be out of the stock as soon as possible.

Remember what I said at the beginning of this chapter. You should have three numbers when entering the market: the entry price, a stop price, and a target selling price. Before you enter the market, you need to know when to get out.

As a day trader, you may also need a time target. It could be one hour, but more than likely you will exit by the end of the day.

And now, based on hundreds of interviews with traders and personal experience, I'm going to introduce you to my five selling guidelines. Use the ones that make sense to you and ignore the rest.

SET FLEXIBLE PRICE TARGETS

Setting price targets can be challenging. On one hand, you want to set realistic price targets based on technical analysis. On the other hand, you must be flexible in case the market doesn't cooperate. Nevertheless, the exact target price is a personal choice.

Whatever you do, don't refuse to take profits because your profit target fell a few quarters short. It happens a lot: traders will refuse to take a profit because they want to squeeze a few more pennies out of a winning stock. And then, just like that, the stock reverses and they lose all their profits! (Not if they use trailing stops, however). As a day trader, you take the profits and run—what I call hit and run trading.

SELL WHEN YOU SEE THAT FIRST COCKROACH

The popular cockroach theory applies to almost anything in life, but especially to trading. In the trading world, it means that if you see or hear problems about a stock you own, assume that's just the beginning. In other words, when you see one cockroach, there are probably many hiding in the background that you can't see.

As a day trader, you'll have to react quickly if there's bad news about a company, or perhaps in that sector. Don't make the common investor mistake of "hoping" that the negative news will pass. More than likely, more bad news will follow.

In addition to the cockroach theory, follow this advice: "When in doubt, get out." One trader told me that as soon as you first think about selling, that's when you should sell. When you're unsure about a stock or have any doubts, either get out completely or reduce your position. Don't forget that you can always repurchase the stock tomorrow.

WATCH OUT FOR EMOTIONAL SELL SIGNALS

This is my personal favorite because I've seen it so often in myself and other traders. As soon as you're counting your profits, giving high fives to your friends, or telling everyone you're a stock market genius, that's the time to sell, or enter a trailing stop-loss order.

In my previous book, *Understanding Options* (McGraw-Hill, 2006), I wrote about a rookie friend of mine who made $130,000 in options profits in one day, but didn't sell because he was certain the underlying stock was going even higher.

Obviously, greed was the culprit, but he didn't recognize it until later that week when he lost all his profits and more. As I said earlier, it is extremely painful to turn a profit into a loss. I don't think my friend ever did recover from his mistake.

Note: By the way, if you find that you're getting too emotional about trading, perhaps that's a signal you need a break, or to find another way to make money. It's not easy to sit and stare at a computer screen, so I recommend taking numerous breaks from trading when you have no open orders or positions. In addition, if you have a series of bad trades, and your confidence is low, that is another signal you need to exercise, take a vacation, or do something besides trading for a while. Controlling emotions is essential if you are going to day trade.

SCALING OUT OF POSITIONS

When it comes to selling stocks, everyone has a different strategy. Some traders like to sell all of their shares in a single trade. Others prefer to *scale* out of a position, that is, sell part of a position, perhaps half, and sell more as profit increases.

The advantage of scaling out is that some profits are captured immediately. The disadvantage is that it can eat up commissions and, for some, it's challenging to juggle multiple trades. If you don't handle scaling properly, you'd be better off getting out of the trade all at once. Perhaps the best advice is to practice scaling out of a position to gain experience.

Scaling is one of the reasons why professional traders prefer to use "per share" commissions rather than per trade. If you're constantly scaling in and out of a position, those per trade transaction costs can be costly, whereas per share transactions are less expensive.

By the way, scaling *into* a position may make more sense to beginner traders. Instead of buying the entire 100 shares at once, begin by buying only 50 shares. Then if the trade goes your way, you can buy the other 50 shares.

NEVER TURN A LOSS INTO AN INVESTMENT

One mistake you should never make is turning a losing stock into an investment, in other words, holding a stock overnight hoping that it will come back. It almost never does! As a day trader, when you have a losing stock, sell that loser before the end of the day. That's one of the best ways to limit losses.

How to Sell

Now that you've learned some selling guidelines, let's go ahead and sell our stock for a gain (in this example). We'll open up our trading screen and take a look at the current bid and ask price (see **Figure 5.4**):

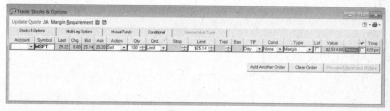

FIG 5.4: Sell Order Screen   For illustrative purposes only. Source: Fidelity Investments. © 2010 FMR LLC. All rights reserved. Used by permission.

After buying Microsoft for $24.00 per share, we will now sell the stock at the current bid price of $25.14. Our gain is 1.14 points x 100 shares for an approximate total of $114.

Although we could have sold the stock for a few pennies higher than the current bid price, we decided not to quibble over pennies, and to sell for a 1-point gain. After clicking on the Preview button to make sure the order is accurate, we place the order and within seconds, it's filled.

If you're dreaming of even bigger profits, first learn the basics. The purpose of these relatively small trades is to build your self-confidence, to learn the nuances of order entries and exits, and to manage risk. This is the cost of your tuition. By using small share sizes and avoiding margin, you can learn valuable lessons while not putting much of your entire portfolio at risk.

Trading Options

As an informed trader, it is important to learn how to buy and sell options. You can use options to protect or hedge your stock portfolio, to speculate, and to generate income. Let's briefly go over three basic option strategies.

SELLING COVERED CALLS

Basically, while holding a long position in an underlying stock, an investor will sell (or write) covered calls on those shares in order to receive income.

Let's say you own 100 shares of XYZ. You then sell 1 call option (1 call is equivalent to 100 shares of stock) to an option buyer. The buyer pays a premium (cash) for the rights to those 100 shares at an agreed-upon price (strike price). You get the cash up front while the option buyer receives the right to buy that stock.

Example: you own XYZ Corporation, which is currently $33 per share. You sell 1 covered call at a strike price of $35 per share. Why sell an option? For the money. The cash premium (the amount depends on the call option price, which constantly changes) is yours to keep. If the stock price rises within a certain time period, (which could be anywhere from days to years), you may be required to sell the shares. That happens when the stock is above $35 when expiration arrives. On the other hand, if the stock drops in price, the option will expire worthless but you still keep the premium. Also, because you still own the stock, you may have unrealized losses on the stock. Nevertheless, the premium you received will help offset the losses.

This strategy, which is flexible and costs little, has been used for years to generate extra income or cash flow. In a way, you're renting your stocks to other people and they pay you for the privilege. The strategy has a dual purpose: to enhance earnings and offer you some protection against loss.

Some people will buy specific stocks just so they can receive cash up front (premium). Underlying stocks that are neutral to slightly bullish are considered ideal for the covered call strategy.

There are risks. For example, if the underlying stock falls more than the value of the covered call you sold, then you are not protected. That is why I suggest you sell covered calls on stocks that are not very volatile.

BUYING OPTIONS FOR SPECULATION

One of the reasons that some traders buy options is to speculate. Most speculators probably lose money, although no one is sure of the exact percentage. To speculate, you can either buy puts (you believe the underlying stock is going down), or calls (you believe the underlying stock is going up). Buying calls and puts work the same way, although you buy them for completely different reasons.

When you buy a call, you're expecting the underlying stock to rise in price; therefore, buying calls is a bullish strategy. To profit, the call buyer has to be correct about the direction and the timing.

Example of Buying a Call:

1. You buy 1 March 20 call option of Daytrader, Inc. The option has a strike price of 20 and expires the third Friday in March. It costs $3.30 per contract for a total cost of $330 plus commission.
2. If Daytrader, Inc. moves above $20 a share (the strike price), the option becomes more valuable. The higher the stock moves above the strike price, the more the option is worth.
3. If the option is well above the strike price on or before the expiration date (third Friday in March), it is likely you can sell the

option for a profit. If the option is at or below the strike price before the expiration date, you will have a loss. (However, there is always the remote chance the underlying stock will move higher very quickly and turn this into a profit).

The main benefit of buying calls is that you can speculate on stocks that you don't own, and the cost can be relatively inexpensive. Also, with calls the most you can lose is what you invested, and not more. Another advantage is that buying calls is often less risky than owning stocks, especially if the stock goes down, not up.

Because some call and put options are so volatile, speculating with them is often more difficult than buying or selling stocks. Nevertheless, for those who want to speculate, options are a fascinating investment, even though they do take some time to fully understand.

HEDGING WITH OPTIONS

Rather than buying calls, you can also buy puts. There are two main reasons to buy puts. One is for speculation. The other is for protection. For example, a popular hedge strategy is buying protective puts. The protective put acts like insurance for your long positions. Buying a put for this reason is similar to buying insurance for your house before an approaching hurricane.

You might wonder why you don't just enter a stop-loss or sell the stock you own. Joe Harwood, manager of the Options Industry Council (OIC) help desk, explains: "What if there is a trading halt and the stock opens drastically lower?" Or, he says, "Perhaps you own an IPO or are with a company that has selling restrictions. Also, shareholders might want to protect unrealized gains for tax purposes, especially if a stock has risen a lot. If the stock drops, the put might increase in value, which would offset part of the loss in the stock."

Harwood says buying puts is not always cheap, but they are an effective way to protect the downside. "This is one way to hedge your portfolio. It will cost money and take away from your overall return, but maybe it will help you protect your investment," he adds.

Nevertheless, there are a number of factors that must be considered before buying a protective put. Author Mark Wolfinger, who publishes the Options for Rookies.com blog, agrees that buying puts is a reasonable strategy, but with some caveats. "Protective puts are fine when the puts are relatively inexpensive," he says.

Although Wolfinger recognizes protective puts make sense for some, his biggest objection is the cost. "There is a point where logical investors will recognize they are paying too much. I don't have that number, but if it costs 20 or 30 percent per year to protect stock, it's too expensive because there is little chance of earning a profit by holding the stock. If you can do it for 5 percent a year, then I'd consider it."

He says that some people will buy protective puts continuously, renewing them every three months. "During a crash, for example, protective puts work, but the cost can be very high. To earn a profit, the stock has to rise by that 20 percent to overcome the cost of insurance. That is unlikely to happen." The best, and simplest, hedge, he says, would have been to sell some stock.

After-Hours Market

The after-hours (or extended) market is the Wild West of electronic trading. This is where mostly professional traders go to trade after the regular market closes at 4:00 P.M. (ET). The after-hours market closes at 8 P.M. (ET).

If you're a rookie trader, the after-hours market is not the kind of place you want to visit very often. Although useful for pros, it can be intimidating for rookies.

Unlike in the regular market, the spreads between the bid and ask are often very wide—sometimes ridiculously so. Why? Because there are few buyers and sellers who are willing to display their bids and offers. Traders use electronic communication networks (ECNs) to display those bids and offers.

ECNs act as electronic middlemen, using a network of computers that work behind the scenes to match buy and sell orders. If you make the mistake of placing a trade after hours without knowing the fair price, you could lose money. If you do participate, you must absolutely use a limit order (an order to a brokerage firm that specifies a specific price to buy or sell a security) Using limit orders is one way of protecting uninformed traders from getting really bad prices. Even if you do use a limit order, however, it's hard to know what a fair price is—another reason why after-hours trading is a difficult trading environment.

The after-hours market also suffers from a lack of liquidity, which means that it's difficult to get into or out of a stock. Unlike in the regular market, where billions of shares are traded every day, only a few million are traded afterhours.

If you participate in the after-hours market, be certain you understand the rules. Ask your brokerage firm for guidance. Keep in mind that some rules that are in place during regular market hours aren't required afterhours.

In general, the after-hour market is too risky for rookie traders, another reason why this session is sometimes referred to as "AH" or "Amateur Hour." Because of the wild price swings and wide spreads, I recommend that you first learn about the regular market.

PART 2

WHAT IT'S REALLY LIKE TO DAY TRADE

Congratulations! You've finished Part 1, which included the mechanics of day trading, which, while important, are only one small part of the process. To succeed as a day trader, you must be disciplined and consistently follow a series of buying and selling rules. If you're consistently ignoring your own rules of when to enter or exit, or how to manage a position, you're not very disciplined.

One thing you should know about being a new trader: you're going to lose money. That's right, during a typical day or week, you'll probably have more losing trades than winning trades. It's the price you pay for being a rookie. I know that some new traders enter the market already anticipating they'll make $200 or $500 every week or every day. I'm here to tell you that is simply not a realistic goal. If you can make 20 percent in a year, you're beating the vast majority of professional traders. In fact, after the first year, if you still have enough money to continue trading, that would be fantastic. By then, you'll have a PhD in making mistakes, the degree almost every trader earns during his or her first year.

Beginning now, I'm going to take you into the trenches with day traders, so you can learn how to use all of these tools to make profitable trades.

Chapter 6:
One Bad Trade

Because I wanted to be different from other authors, I decided to give you a real-life idea of what it's like to make a really bad trade. If I simply listed The Rules, as most authors do, you wouldn't experience what it's really like to be an undisciplined trader.

Therefore, I wrote this chapter as a narrative, based on a mostly true story of one rookie trader. Unfortunately, at one time or another, thousands of other traders have had similar experiences. I'm hoping that by reading about his mistakes, you can avoid repeating them. In reality, most traders have to learn the hard lessons for themselves. My goal is to save you from such experiences.

Although Hal (not his real name) learned a lot about the stock market from his family, he had only made a handful of trades, mostly investments in well-known companies like IBM or Apple.

As a waiter at a local restaurant in 2007, Hal had heard from the other servers and some customers that it was possible to make far more than 10 percent a year trading in stocks. In fact, other waiters claimed that they were making $200 to $300 per day by day trading from their homes. To earn $200 a day, or $50,000 a year, seemed like a dream to Hal. He could quit working full-time and concentrate on making money, all from the comfort of his own home.

The more Hal thought about trading, the more he liked the idea. When one waiter pulled up in a brand new car, made possible by trading, Hal was convinced to give it a try. He was going to increase his income by trading stocks. He began by watching financial television programs, monitoring online chat rooms, and reading Internet blogs. He even read a couple of trading books.

The Tip

At work, Hal got into a conversation with a regular customer, Mr. Morgan (not his real name), who seemed like he had a lot of money. Mr. Morgan drove a nice car and had an oceanfront condominium. Mr. Morgan told Hal that he could make a really nice living trading stocks. "I trade stocks for a living," Mr. Morgan explained. "I'm a professional day trader."

The stock market had been going up for a number of years but had been extremely volatile over the last few months. For many traders, this seemed like a good time to scoop up bargains. Hal had his eye on a low-priced stock that he could get for only $7 per share. He immediately told Mr. Morgan about his idea.

"Stay away from stocks like that," Mr. Morgan said. "It has no volume and a poor history."

Hal was eager to participate in the market. "So what do you recommend?"

"I'm associated with a group of professional traders," Mr. Morgan said, "but first you have to promise not to tell anyone about my trades."

"I promise," Hal said.

"Okay, we really like Citigroup for a position trade," he said, almost in a whisper. "It was trading at $50 per share but now it's at $38. We think this is a good buying opportunity."

Hal was impressed with Citigroup, one of the most well-known banks in the country. Hal went on the Internet and researched what other analysts thought about this company. The consensus seemed positive. Everyone liked it. At $38 per share, Citicorp seemed like a bargain.

"How many shares should I buy?" Hal asked.

"That's up to you," Mr. Morgan said. "I bought 4,000 shares for my account."

Four thousand shares! That would cost Hal $152,000, an impossible amount of money for him to obtain.

"What if I bought 1,000 shares?" Hal asked.

"That's a good start," Mr. Morgan replied. "We expect it to go back to $50 per share in the near future."

That would be a 12-point gain! Hal relished the idea of making $12,000 in a few weeks. He could never make that kind of money waiting on tables.

Hal was tired of being a waiter and was eager to make a killing in the stock market. Since he worked nights, he could trade during the day and still make it to work before his night shift started.

Hal's biggest problem was funding his account. He had already saved up $5,000, but he needed a lot more money to buy 1,000 shares at $38. First, he charged $5,000 on his credit card. Then he begged his parents for money, but his father had a better idea. He agreed to add Hal to his trading account, as long as Hal split the profits. The two men drove to the brokerage firm and signed the required application forms. Hal was pleased when he had access to over $100,000 on margin, more than enough money to buy 1,000 shares of Citicorp.

That weekend, Hal went to the bookstore and bought a handful of trading books. He also bought a huge 21-inch monitor and attached it to his computer with two top-of-the-line surge protectors. He also bought copies of *Investor's Business Daily*, *The Wall Street Journal*, and *Barron's*. He was ready and willing to be a trader.

After Hal's shift ended late Sunday night, he went to sleep, waking up around 9:00 A.M., eager to place his first trade. He was excited about the prospect of making a quick $12,000. He called his girlfriend and told her that after he sold his stocks for a profit, they were going to Paris next summer.

Hal opened up the brokerage firm's software and was dazzled by the charts and other information on the screens. It looked like fun, but it was confusing. He called the brokerage for help with the entry screens and also sent Mr. Morgan an e-mail a couple of times before the market opened.

The Rise

Hal placed his first trade at 9:40 A.M., ten minutes after the market opened. Citicorp spiked up a few points right at the beginning, which convinced Hal that the stock was going even higher. He entered a market order for 1,000 shares as Citicorp continued to move. He bought 1,000 shares at $40.50. Cost: $40,500.

At first, Citicorp zoomed up another two points, to $42.08, giving Hal an unrealized profit of over $1,500. That was more money than he ever made in one day as a waiter. He thought about selling, but he wanted a homerun, not a single. "To make big money, you have to bet big money," he told himself.

As the market closed for the day, Hal decided to hold the stock overnight, thrilled that he had still had a $1,500 profit in one day.

That night, Hal's confidence in Citicorp grew as he read positive articles about the company. One guy on TV ranted about Citicorp for over ten minutes, and yelled into the cameras that the stock was a "buy, buy, buy." The only negative articles Hal found was about the entire financial sector, which seemed somewhat weak. But Hal read an article that claimed that Citicorp was immune to a possible banking crisis.

That night, Hal called his mother and told her he was going to get rich. His father was also pleased with his son's success.

His girlfriend stopped by to look at his computer monitor. "You should have sold it," she suggested. "I would have taken the money."

Hal frowned. "You don't know anything about the stock market."

Market Mayhem

Over the next few weeks, the market fell by more than 1 percent, and so did Citicorp. In fact, Citicorp dropped by 7 points (more than 15 percent) to approximately $35. His $1,500 gain had turned into a $5,000 loss.

He called Mr. Morgan for advice.

"We're buying more," Mr. Morgan said. "Citi hasn't been this low in years. It's too cheap to sell."

"I don't know if I can afford to buy more shares," Hal said.

"If you don't buy more shares, you'll be making the biggest financial mistake of your life!" Mr. Morgan screamed into the phone.

"Okay, okay," Hal replied, intimidated by Mr. Morgan's loud voice. So Hal placed another market order for another 1,000 shares. He was filled at approximately $36 per share for a total cost of $36,000. He had now invested over $75,000 in Citicorp stock.

For the next few weeks, Hal was obsessed with Citicorp, and so was his entire family. They were cheering the stock on, and no one could talk about anything else.

"If this stock goes to $50," Hal promised his girlfriend, "We're going to have the biggest party ever." Copying the antics of the host of a popular financial program, using a blue marker, Hal wrote the stock symbol—C—on every knuckle.

All month, Citicorp seesawed between $35 and $37 per share. Hal saw Mr. Morgan at the restaurant a couple of times but there was no news. "Sometimes you just have to wait," Mr. Morgan said, shrugging his shoulders.

Over the next few months, the stock market fell by more than 3 percent, but Citicorp did even worse, falling to $25. When Hal looked at the computer screen, he felt dizzy. Now he and his father were down over $25,000. "I can't believe this," Hal groaned.

He called Mr. Morgan, who told him that what happened to the market was an unusual event. "You can't plan for the unexpected," he told him. "Just sit tight. It will come back."

Hal was hopeful he could get back to even. He wanted his money back.

A few months later, Citicorp fell by another 5 points. Hal had more than $37,000 in losses, and now owed the brokerage firm for the margin he used. Hal continuously called Mr. Morgan but there was no answer. Finally, he reached him late one night.

"Mr. Morgan, what should we do about Citicorp? It's $20 per share. I'm getting killed."

"Oh, Citicorp. I sold that stock a month ago," Mr. Morgan snapped. "And don't ever call me again!"

Late that night, Hal received a phone call from his father. "I got a margin call from the broker this afternoon," he said. "I have to add more money within twenty-four hours or they're going to sell all the shares. I feel sick." Hal felt even worse.

The next morning, Hal was hoping that Citicorp would bounce back, but it continued to fall. His father called Hal. "I sold it," he said. "We got creamed on that stock."

By the time the position was liquidated, with commissions and charges, Hal and his father had lost over $45,000. Hal personally owed $10,000 in credit card charges.

Lessons Learned

Later that night, Hal sat down and wrote down all of the mistakes he and his father had made with Citicorp. He was shocked at what he did. "How could I have been so stupid?" he thought.

WHAT WENT WRONG

Ironically, most of the worst mistakes Hal made occurred before he placed his first trade. The first financial mistake Hal made was buying a stock based on a tip, even from a so-called financial professional like Mr. Morgan. Hal thought that Mr. Morgan was smarter than the market, a deadly error. Tipsters like Mr. Morgan are everywhere, and it costs them nothing to give out free advice. The only antidote to listening to stock tips from so-called trading experts is to keep your ears shut, and not pay attention.

Lesson #1:
Don't listen to tips.

Hal borrowed money from his credit card to fund his account, a serious money management mistake. Even with his father's help, Hal was trading with money he couldn't afford to lose, which should have forced him to be extra careful. Instead, he took unnecessary risks. The pressure to pay back his family and make a big trade was tremendous. The pros call this trading with "scared money."

Lesson #2:
Don't borrow money to fund an account, and don't take extra risks under any circumstances.

Hal believed that to make big money, he had to bet big money. This myth is perpetuated to separate people from their money. Hal should have invested a small amount of money, especially when he was first starting as a trader. He didn't anticipate that when you bet big, you can lose big, too.

Lesson #3:
Manage money carefully. Be aware of how much money can be lost and be certain you can afford that loss.

Based on the advice he heard from Mr. Morgan, Hal entered the market with unrealistically high expectations. For example, Mr. Morgan lured Hal into the trade by saying that Citicorp "should" be at $50 per share. The market doesn't care what Mr. Morgan or anyone thinks. There is no "should" when it comes to the market; anything is possible. As Hal learned the hard way, the market always has the final word.

Lesson #4:
The market is always right.

Hal anticipated huge profits for this trade. Yes, it's true that Hal "could" have made $10,000 in profits or more, but he also failed to anticipate potential losses. He also assumed he could make $50,000 every year trading stocks. Unfortunately, he didn't account for any of the losing days.

Lesson #5:
Enter the market with realistic expectations, and don't count on pretend profits.

ENTERING THE MARKET

These mistakes could have been avoided if Hal had created a set of rules and a trading plan before entering the market. The rules should have been posted in clear view: an entry price, an exit price, and a stop-loss. Because Hal didn't have any rules, he ended up making impulsive trades without a clue what he was doing.

Lesson #6:
Create a trading plan and follow rules.

Instead of asking "How much can I make?" Hal should have immediately asked Mr. Morgan, "How much can I lose?" This would have forced Hal to use stop-losses and taken other steps to protect his principal. If he were more knowledgeable, he might have set price alerts. Hal was trading with over $75,000 and didn't plan for a worst-case scenario.

Lesson #7:
Use stop-losses or price alerts.

Hal also should have followed a basic money management rule: don't risk more than a certain amount of your total account equity on any one trade. For example, some traders won't risk more than 2 percent of their portfolio. For retail day traders, however, 2 percent might not be realistic. The "2-percent rule" is a useful guideline, but is not set in stone. Nevertheless, with experience, you can create your own percentage. Sadly, Hal didn't know he should decide in advance how much to risk on his total account until it was too late. For example, if he had risked only 500 shares and included a stop-loss, Hal would have been protected.

Lesson #8:
Set a stop-loss and don't risk more
than a predetermined sum on any one trade.

Perhaps Hal's biggest mistake was thinking that his secret weapon, Mr. Morgan, would keep him out of trouble. Because Hal thought that this was a risk-free trade, he took incredibly huge chances.

Lesson #9:
There's no such thing as a risk-free trade.

Once Hal began thinking of all the money he "could" earn, greed clouded his judgment. It's not surprising what happened to

Hal. As he learned the hard way, a lack of knowledge combined with unrealistic expectations and greed can do strange things to people. Remember this: as a day trader, you have to take what the market gives you, not what you think you deserve.

Lesson #10:
Have reasonable target goals and book profits when goals are reached.

PLACING THE ORDER

Amazingly, all of these mistakes were made before Hal even placed his first trade. He was doomed from the start, but he also made some mistakes when he placed the order.

For example, Hal bought Citicorp at the market open. Because stocks occasionally gap up on the first trade of the day, entering orders at that time can often result in bad fills. It's better to wait at least fifteen minutes before placing a trade, especially if you're a rookie. You have all day to trade, so be patient.

Lesson #11:
Avoid trading during the first fifteen minutes after the market opens.

Another warning sign Hal didn't heed was the rush of excitement he felt as he placed his first trade. "Trading should be as emotional as dropping off the laundry at the dry cleaner," quipped one professional trader. You deserve to feel pleased, however, when you look at a profitable monthly or quarterly return.

Lesson #12:
Learn how to trade without emotion.

Unfortunately, Hal was so eager to buy Citicorp he entered a market order, resulting in an especially bad fill. He lost over a point per share on that trade alone, costing him more than $1,000. Hal should have entered a limit order and taken control of the trade, telling the market the price he was willing to pay. Instead, Hal rushed into the trade without thinking, letting the market decide on the price.

Lesson #13:
The market is like an auction;
use limit orders to get a more competitive price.

In addition to using limit orders, Hal could have scaled into the trade with a hundred shares. Scaling in can be an effective way to test the market environment. Although initially Citicorp rose, the next day's drop was a warning sign. Hal would have been wise to start with fewer shares. Trading with 1,000 shares at one time was risky.

Lesson #14:
Consider scaling into a trade with fewer shares.

Finally, Hal was destined to fail because he was woefully unprepared for psychological warfare. Once Hal entered the market, he was trading with sharks, and he was the fish chum. Reading a couple of books and financial newspapers about the market did not prepare him for the financial battle of his life. If anything, Hal should have spent weeks, if not months, practicing and preparing for his first trade.

Lesson #15:
Prepare in advance before placing your first trade.
Practice trading.

MANAGING THE TRADE

Hal also made additional mistakes after he bought Citicorp. At first it rose by 2 points. He didn't realize that managing winning stocks is often as challenging as handling losing stocks. The most important goal for a trader is to manage risk so losses don't get too large. Although blinded by his 2-point gain, Hal should have set a trailing stop-loss based on the higher price.

Hal also bragged to his parents and girlfriend about his trading abilities, a flashing red warning signal. The feeling of making $1,500 in minutes was intoxicating, but also dangerous to his portfolio. After making that much money, Hal was deceived into thinking that trading was easy.

Lesson #16:
Avoid greed by using stop-losses.

In fact, Hal was so pleased with his so-called trading ability he left the house at one point, putting his account on autopilot. Some novice traders have been known to go on extended vacations after placing a trade, only to return to a nearly empty account.

Lesson #17:
Never take your eye off of an active trade.

EXITING THE TRADE

A glaring psychological sell signal was flashed when Hal wrote the letter C on his knuckles. Once Hal fell in love with this stock, he lost all objectivity. He stopped paying attention to negative newspaper articles, listening only to people who supported his view. With that much money at stake, Hal should have closely monitored the market using technical indicators. Once Hal became the company's cheerleader, it was too painful to sell. Rather than relying on the facts to make trading decisions, he relied on hope, and on Mr. Morgan.

Lesson #18:
Don't fall in love with a stock.

Because Hal no longer had a neutral view of the stock, he did not prepare for a worst-case scenario. Simply put, he had no clue what to do if he, or Mr. Morgan, was wrong. Some traders assume a stock is a turkey unless proven otherwise. To Hal, it was inconceivable that such a well-known and powerful company's stock could plunge. As a result, Hal continued to watch helplessly without entering a stop-loss. If he had, his portfolio could have been saved and the damage might have been minimal.

Lesson #19:
Plan for worst-case scenarios by using stop-loss orders.

When the stock rallied the first day, Hal stopped paying attention to the overall market and Citicorp's sector, the financials. If Hal had looked, he would have noticed that both were struggling.

Lesson #20:
Study the overall market and individual sectors for clues.

If Hal had studied the market, he might have noticed that several key indicators, such as moving averages, were giving out warning signals. For example, Citicorp, and the overall stock market, was trading well below its 200-day and 100-day moving averages, a big warning sign. Also, going long in a potential bear market wasn't the wisest decision. The only indicator that Hal followed was Mr. Morgan, a disastrous mistake.

Lesson #21:
Use technical indicators.

When Citicorp fell by 5 points, Hal panicked. Instead of getting out with a relatively small loss, he made a dreadful mistake: he bought more shares, doubling down on his losing position. Because of a range of emotions, inexperience, and bad advice, Hal now risked a financial Armageddon. An experienced trader would have taken the loss and looked for other opportunities. Hal, on the other hand, couldn't let go.

Lesson #22:
You must be willing to accept some losses.

Although many traders can handle winners, they often have no idea what to do about losers. The pressure on Hal to succeed as a trader was overwhelming, not only financially but emotionally as well. The loss of money, which represented all of his hopes, dreams, and self-esteem, caused Hal to make impulsive decisions. Once the stock didn't perform as expected, he should have reevaluated the trade and exited immediately.

In Hal's mind, this one bad trade had to be successful or he'd lose the respect of his family, the love of his girlfriend, and his self-esteem. It was not surprising that he reacted in fear when the stock didn't perform as expected.

Lesson #23: Learn how to lose before you win.

Another huge mistake Hal made was overtrading. Once Citicorp didn't go his way, instead of calmly exiting the position, he traded again. The best traders patiently wait for other, more profitable stocks. Hal was so anxious to recover losses he made what is called a revenge trade.

Lesson #24:
Be patient and wait for profitable trading opportunities.

Perhaps the most dangerous error of all was Hal's misuse of margin. With his father's help, his account was boosted to $100,000. Hal and his father were emotionally unprepared to handle that much money. They didn't understand how leverage increases losses on the way down. In the hands of an experienced trader, leverage can be a very powerful tool. In the hands of a rookie trader like Hal, it can wipe out an account.

Lesson #25:
Rookie traders should avoid using margin.

Another error Hal made was changing his strategy from a trade into an investment. When Citicorp fell in price, instead of selling immediately for a relatively small loss, he waited for the stock to come back to even. In addition, once the stock went against him, he should not have taken the position home. After Hal's original plan didn't work out, and losses were multiplying, getting out completely was the only solution.

Lesson #26:
Cut your losses at a predetermined price,
and sell when the original plan stops working.

If Hal had spent as much time thinking of selling as he did of buying, he may have escaped this trade with a profit. Hal had no idea when to sell and was too inexperienced to realize that 2 points was the most the market would ever give him on this trade. (Even if he did sell for a gain, as an amateur, Hal might have complained that he "could have, would have, and should have" made more money on the trade. That's another reason why he needed a trailing stop).

Lesson #27:
Have a selling plan before you buy.

In fact, Hal's only selling plan was to wait for Mr. Morgan to tell him what to do. By blindly relying on Mr. Morgan for all trading decisions, Hal only traded for a day. If he had learned how to find his own stocks and make his own decisions, he could have traded for a lifetime.

Lesson #28:
Think for yourself.

Even more dangerous to Hal's trading account and self-esteem, Hal allowed Mr. Morgan to bully and scream at him to buy a stock. When someone yells at you to buy or sell a stock, it might be better to do the opposite. At the very least, Hal should have taken the time to study and think, but he was too emotionally involved. Hal could have sought a second opinion from a trusted professional. As it turned out, however, Mr. Morgan didn't care about Hal or how much money he made or lost.

Lesson #29:
Don't let someone pressure you into a trade.

To Hal's credit, he finally sold. He realized how ridiculously risky the trade was, and got out before his father's account was totally destroyed. It actually could have been much worse. Over the next several months, Citicorp eventually fell below $4 per share, where it remained for several years.

If the stock of one of the largest and most powerful banks could lose 90 percent of its value, then you know that anything is possible in the stock market. It took Hal years to pay back all of the money he borrowed.

Lesson #30:
Anything is possible in the stock market.

If Hal had kept a journal of all of the mistakes he made on his one bad trade, he could have learned enough lessons to last a lifetime. Because he didn't record why and when he bought the stock, the number of shares, and his target price, he was trading emotionally. Without the benefit of keeping a journal, he could repeat many of the same mistakes.

Lesson #31:
Keep a journal of all trades.

NEVER AGAIN

For months, Hal was angry at himself and Mr. Morgan. "How could I be so stupid?" he repeatedly said to himself. Eventually, Hal took full responsibility for his bad trade. After all, if Hal had more self-confidence and knowledge about the market, he would have ignored Mr. Morgan's tips and temper tantrum.

A little gossip: Mr. Morgan never talked to Hal again. Occasionally, Hal saw Mr. Morgan walking near the bookstore or the mall, but Mr. Morgan quickly ran in the opposite direction, mumbling to himself, "Uhhhooohhhh, uhhhhohhhh." He probably thought that Hal was still angry, but Hal wasn't at all.

They never spoke again but it didn't matter. The lessons that Hal learned from that one bad trade helped him not only in the stock market, but in life.

Looking back, many of Hal's trading errors could be traced to low self-esteem, inadequate knowledge, and inexperience. Most important, Hal learned to trust his own judgment when it came to the stock market, or with any decision. It's reasonable to listen to other people, but don't rely on them when making the final decision. Many traders don't know what they're talking about.

Lesson #32:
Trust yourself.

Even after losing so much money, Hal didn't give up. For the next year, he diligently studied the stock market and became much more knowledgeable. After he pays back what he owes to his family, he plans to re-enter the market, slowly and carefully, and with a lot less money.

"I won't make the same mistakes," he wrote in his journal.

He paid a high price, but, ironically, the lessons he learned from one bad trade were the best thing that ever happened to him.

Lesson #33:
Turn lemons into lemonade.

Live to Trade Another Day

I hope that this narrative gave you some insights into how novice traders can lose their entire portfolio on one bad trade. As you can see, trading is an incredibly emotional experience, similar to riding a roller coaster with your pockets full of cash. As day traders, it can be even more intense.

As I said before, your initial goal is to learn how to be a good trader, not necessarily to make money. Most important, always take steps to protect your portfolio: preserving your capital is your number one goal. There will always be more trading opportunities, but only as long as you can remain in the game.

After several months of trading, you'll have a much better idea whether trading is a good fit for you. As you now know, successful trading involves mastering money and emotions. If you're unable to manage both, then you may want to re-evaluate whether you should keep trading. Although the mechanics of trading can be learned fairly easily, making lightning-fast decisions while juggling thousands of dollars is a huge challenge. You better love what you're doing, or look for another way to make a living.

High-Frequency Trading

High-frequency traders (HFT) are the ultimate day traders. They use high-speed computers to automatically send out millions of orders, probing and scalping for pennies, which add up to billions of dollars in profits every year. It's been reported that high-speed trading firms account for more than 70 percent of the trading volume on some days.

Retail day traders cannot compete with high-frequency traders or the hundreds of millions of dollars in technology they own, including huge bandwidth that allows HFTs to make transactions in nanoseconds.

Proponents of high-frequency trading claim that these traders add liquidity to the market—in other words, they make it easier for others to buy share size. These traders claim they have helped narrow spreads and lowered volatility. Unfortunately, although HFTs act almost like market makers and specialists, they do not have to follow the strict requirements of keeping a fair and orderly market. This was quite apparent on May 6, 2010, when these traders simply pulled all of their bids when the first flash crash occurred.

One of the most controversial strategies used by some high-frequency traders is *flash trading*. This strategy allows traders to "ping" other large market participants for a quick 30-second peak at their outstanding orders. This gives the high-frequency traders insights into order flow, allowing them to change their orders before they're filled.

For example, if an HFT notices a sudden flurry of buying interest in a particular stock, they could add to the position or sell the stock short. Gaining a glimpse into another participant's order book is about as close to "front running" (the unethical practice of making a trade based on advance knowledge) as one can get.

Not all HFTs use flash trading, but the strategy is controversial. When the first flash crash occurred in 2010, the market plunged by over 600 points within minutes, only to regain almost all of the points lost. According to the Security and Exchange Commission (SEC) and the Commodity Futures Trade Commission (CFTC), who issued a joint report, the flash crash was caused by a computerized trading program that automatically sold 35,000 E-mini S&P futures contracts.

Nevertheless, the rapid and sudden selling was disturbing to investors, who began pulling money out of the stock market and putting it into bonds. For some investors, flash-trading tactics makes the market seem like a rigged game.

Although high-frequency trading can add liquidity to the market, if Main Street investors lose confidence in the financial markets and refuse to invest, then all that increased volume means little. Although computerization of orders began decades ago with a variety of proprietary programs (some claim the 1987 crash was caused by program traders), the flash crash was the first time the public got a real glimpse into what is happening behind the scenes.

Because the rules surrounding high-frequency trading are rather loose, more firms are creating multimillion-dollar computer systems with sophisticated algorithms designed to take even more market share. Until rules are put into place to limit some of these activities, the retail investor may not choose to participate. Even the perception of an unfair system can be harmful to a market that is supposed to level the playing field for investors. As a result of the damage caused by the flash crash, the SEC proposed a new rule that prohibits all markets from displaying flash orders. The goal, of course, is to prevent another flash crash.

Chapter 7: Meeting the Pros

Keep in mind that when you read about day trading in a book, it seems relatively easy, but in real life it's a lot more challenging. That's why it's always educational to visit a day trader's home office, especially when they're willing to share a few of their secrets. To give you a better idea of what really happens behind a day trader's door, I tracked down a handful of professional traders and asked them for advice.

By the time you finish this chapter, you should have learned a few more tricks. After all, getting inside the minds of real traders can be extremely educational. Learning about all the things that can go right, or wrong, can save you time and money.

Toni Turner, Bestselling Author and Trader

Toni Turner is the best-selling author of A Beginner's Guide to Day Trading Online, 2nd Edition, A Beginner's Guide to Short-Term Trading, and Short-Term Trading in the New Stock Market. Her books have been translated into multiple languages, and have also been used as textbooks in personal finance college courses.

An accomplished technical analyst, Turner is well known for her ability to present complicated material in a simplified manner that makes it interesting and enjoyable to learn. She is the president of TrendStar Trading Group, Inc.

LEARN TO READ THE MARKET

Turner says that new traders primarily lose money because they "don't know how to read the markets."

For example, she says "the major indexes might go higher during the day. A new trader might see this is as an opportunity to go long and hold their positions overnight. An experienced trader, however, will see that the market moved higher within a severe downtrend. They'll see the lower highs and lower lows. The beginner won't see those signals and suffer severe losses when the market rolls over."

To see the bigger picture, Turner constantly watches the major indexes on multiple time frames, including daily and weekly charts, even when she is day trading. "Reading the market is like getting lost in a dangerous forest," she says. "An experienced guide will know what signs to look for, see the animal tracks, and find a way out. If an inexperienced person got lost in the forest, he probably wouldn't last the night."

LEARN HOW TO PAPER TRADE

To gain experience, Turner suggests that new traders begin by paper trading. "By paper trading for several months and learning along the way, you gain confidence. Because it's not real, you won't lose money as you're learning the market signs."

Although paper trading is very helpful, Turner says that it's not perfect. "Because your emotions are not on the line when you paper trade," she says, "it's entirely different from trading in the real market. Remember that it's a lot easier when you paper trade because you don't feel any pain when you make mistakes." The key, she says, is to treat paper trading seriously, and not as a game.

READ THE FUTURE

When Turner is day trading, she looks at the S&P 500 E-mini future contracts, which are traded in the S&P pit at the Chicago Mercantile Exchange. She says they act as a leading indicator for the stocks in the S&P 500. "The E-minis will tick higher," she says, "and then the majority of stocks will follow it higher. And if the S&P E-minis go lower, the majority of stocks will go lower. You only get a few seconds warning before this happens, but it's enough time to get in or out of a position."

She says that you can also watch the Nasdaq 100 E-mini futures, which act as leading indicator for Nasdaq stocks. In addition, the mini-sized Dow contract is the leading indicator for the Dow Jones Industrial Average (DJIA).

Turner gets her E-mini quotes from a direct-access broker for a small fee, but agrees that some online brokers may offer them in the future. She says the futures contracts are also displayed on most financial programs or on the web, but day traders need an immediate reading.

HOW TO USE LEVEL II

Although some traders have relied less on Level II quotes in recent years, Turner finds them very helpful for day traders. "I will not trade a stock unless I first look at the Level II screen," she says. "I want to see the personality and character of the stocks that I trade, and Level II gives me clues. I also want to see the spread. If a stock has more than a one- or two-cent spread between the bid and the ask, I will avoid it." The reason? "That's because more than a one- or two-cent spread means I may not be able to enter—or more importantly—exit a trade at the exact price I am targeting," she says. "A wide spread between the bid and ask prices means the market makers are controlling my entries and exits."

She has other criteria about the stocks she buys. They have to be very liquid, for example, trading between 300,000 and half a million shares a day. Volume information is also displayed on traditional quote screens, but Level II goes even deeper.

Turner is well aware of the limitations of Level II, especially given how some market players hide their true intentions by playing games with orders. "Everyone is allowed to slice up their orders," she says, explaining how participants will hide a large order by slicing it into 100-share lots. She laughs and continues. "Sometimes with Level II screens, you can't believe your lying eyes." Even with these caveats, Turner finds Level II useful, particularly for day traders.

To verify what she sees on Level II, Turner also looks at Time and Sales, which displays the actual orders. But even then, some market players have made side arrangements to sell million-share lots, the so-called *shadow market*, which won't show up on Time and Sales. "There are undercurrents of other trades going on that we might not be privy to," she cautions.

PLAN THE TRADE AND TRADE THE PLAN

The stocks that Turner likes to day trade the most are ones that aren't in the spotlight. "The majority of the time, I find it better to avoid stocks that are in the news," she says. "Many times, stocks in the news are the stocks favored by the biggest and baddest high-frequency traders, and I don't care to compete with them for fractions of pennies. I've learned from experience that stocks that are not in the media spotlight may not be as exciting, but can develop orderly patterns, and thus earn me the most profits."

The night before the market opens, or early the next morning, Turner scans through stocks that meet her criteria. She begins by studying the sectors, then makes a watch list of the stocks or exchange-traded funds (ETFs) that are consolidating and appear ready to break out. She often trades ETFs because they are less risky than individual stocks and because they are more diversified. ETFs are traded just like stocks; they provide diversification, and are relatively inexpensive. In addition to using them as a hedge against a portfolio of individual stocks, you can also buy ETFs in specific sectors, countries, or asset classes. In a way, ETFs are similar to buying mutual funds, but without a fund manager. Because of these advantages, many people are huge fans of buying ETFs and have created portfolios to reflect their views of the market or individual stocks.

"One of my best day trading strategies," she adds, "is to find stocks that are in an uptrend on the daily chart. It should be above the 20-day and 50-day moving average. Then I pull up a 15-minute chart with a 10-period and 20-period moving average. As long as the stock is breaking higher, you can use the crossovers of these moving averages to buy and sell."

She looks for the following signals: "When the 10-period moving average crosses above the 20-period moving average, it's a buy signal," she says. "When the 10-period moves below the 20-period moving average, it's a sell signal. This is one of the simplest and most basic strategies, and it works. Try it as a paper trade and see if it works for you."

CAN YOU DAY TRADE PART-TIME?

Turner says it is possible to day trade part-time, but only if you are as knowledgeable as full-time traders. "You can't expect to be a part-time trader if you enter without a full skill set and discipline," she cautions. "It's like a surgeon who only knows how to take out an appendix. If you think you can trade part-time with part-time knowledge, you could get killed in the market."

In addition to having skills and discipline, Turner warns traders about the challenges. "All new traders, and even experienced ones, have to eat a little glass. That's the way it is. That's why it's so important to trade with money you can afford to lose, and to have a cushion." She suggests that new traders not use margin, even when it's available.

To be a successful trader, Turner advises that you "establish a well-thought-out trading plan as soon as you enter a trade. As soon as you enter the trade, place a hard stop—meaning a protective stop with your broker—right away. That keeps you out of trouble more than anything else I know. Your goal at the beginning is to protect your principal and stay even."

John Kurisko, Professional Day Trader

John Kurisko, also known as Day Trader Rock Star, runs a daily video and radio show on *www.daytradingradio.com* that anyone can watch during market hours. Kurisko recalls his early attempts at learning how to day trade. "It was in the early '90s and I was looking for that Holy Grail of trading," he says. "I was going into all these chat rooms and bulletin boards to find direction. Back then, trading from home was just starting to take off."

At the same time, Kurisko says, day trading was like the "wild west of trading. I remember trading CMGI, (now called ModusLink Global Solutions), which was a venture capitalist group. I bought 400 shares and, because I was an inexperienced trader, I went to the mall. When I came back, the market was closed, but the stock was up over 64 points. I couldn't sleep that night. The next day, it went up even more, so by the time I sold that morning, I was $30,000 richer. I had never experienced anything like that, stocks going up 20 and 30 points. Unfortunately, a lot of traders blew up their accounts when it stopped working."

Over time, Kurisko developed a style of trading that focuses on high-probability setups. This criterion is determined by a set of five technical indicators that will set up and show the best risk reward entry for a quality stock in a pullback.

HIGH-PROBABILITY TRADES

One of Kurisko's day trading guidelines is to not make trading too complicated. "Instead of trying to pick a top or bottom, and getting taken out of your position," he suggests, "have the discipline and patience to follow the price trend. Too many people get greedy and want to make something happen."

The key, he suggests, is patiently waiting until there is a high-probability setup. "Many people don't know that one of the secrets of being a successful day trader is being patient."

Unlike many traders, Kurisko is not as comfortable with shorting stocks. "Maybe it's my optimistic personality," he says, "but I don't take both sides of the market. If I see a stock top out, I'll wait until the stock comes to a level where I can go long. For me, shorting is too tough. I don't want to get chopped up trying to find a top."

Specifically, Kurisko's ideal setup is trading high-quality stocks that are pulling back. "For me, a high-probability trade is when the price of a high-quality stock pulls back to the trendline and starts to move up. It's a textbook trade, not gambling. The exciting part is it's such an easy trade when you see it. I could do that trade all day long. All the indicators line up, and you get a bounce. The key is don't get greedy, and then you move on."

Kurisko says it's much easier to buy on a pullback and go with the trend of the market than try to catch the top or bottom. "You need patience and discipline to let the stock come down to an area where it's going to bounce, whether it happens Monday, Tuesday, or Wednesday. You don't chase it. You have your business plan and you wait for stocks to set up. I buy them and I sell them with no emotion. It's an excellent way to make a living."

SCANNING FOR STOCKS TO BUY

Kurisko likes to have a list of stocks to watch, what he calls a focus list. "I scan through hundreds of stocks at night looking for high-probability setups. I mostly look at stocks in the S&P 500 because they are quality stocks that have already been broken into sectors."

He created his own criteria, such as stocks that are pulling down to a trendline. They also have to be above their 200-day moving average. Finally, he scans for a *wedge* (similar to a triangle) pattern. He says you could set up any criteria you want on the scan programs.

"I'm scanning all the time," Kurisko acknowledges. "In my office I have seven screens with over eighty stocks. Then I have charts of the twelve main stocks I'm looking at. I'm constantly looking for divergences and buying spikes." Because Kurisko is constantly on the air, he says, "I have to act as the eyes and ears for my viewers."

Unlike some other traders, Kurisko doesn't use Level II to monitor his focus list. "I never really got into Level II. I didn't like how these ghost orders would suddenly appear and then they'd disappear. What's good about Level II is you can see the 10,000 share orders holding at a certain price level. What's bad is some of these orders aren't real. Also, price action will always show up on the charts before it shows up on Level II."

Therefore, Time and Sales is more useful to Kurisko. "I sometimes look at it to get a feel for the size of the trades going through," he says. "It tells me if day traders or institutional buyers are in the market. If a 10,000-share order is going through, Time and Sales will tell me that."

He also uses basic scanning software to find stocks that meet his criteria. "I might scan for stocks that are between the 20-period and 50-period moving average, or one that is oversold on Stochastics. It keeps me out of the junk. But I wouldn't recommend paying $900 for a program that you can get for $49."

In addition to scanning software, Kurisko also pays extra for news feeds, which he feels gives him an edge. "I want to know if there is breaking news before it's shown on television. By that time it might be too late. Many times I've seen something like the Gross Domestic Product (GDP) being announced a few seconds late. I need to be on top of the news and always be prepared."

KURISKO'S FIVE FAVORITE INDICATORS

"The signals I look for are Stochastics, trendlines, moving averages, support and resistance, and patterns," explains Kurisko. "Starting with Stochastics, I want it to be oversold. Next, I look at the

20-, 50-, and 200-day exponential moving average (EMA). What's great about the indicators is they help let you know when to buy and when to sell."

Kurisko also wants to see recognizable patterns, such as candlestick reversals or an inverted head and shoulders, that match his long-only trading philosophy. He also wants the stock price to be touching support or resistance before he buys or sells.

To make a trade, Kurisko doesn't need all five indicators lined up, but at least three indicators are important. "Once I see the patterns starting to build and the indicators lined up, I'll take the trade," he says.

It's always an added bonus if there are recognizable patterns. "I sometimes don't understand why everyone doesn't see the patterns," he says. "Maybe it takes experience to see the curvatures of the lines and how the market reacts to volume, because I'll see it but others sometimes don't. Studying the pattern should not be a scientific process. It's just there."

The patterns appear on almost any time frame on a chart, from the 1-minute to the daily. "The longer the time frame," Kurisko explains, "the longer you might want to hold it. If I see the pattern show up on a 1-minute chart, then it will be a day trade. But sometimes the pattern crosses all time periods, so you have to be patient to see how it plays out."

Although Kurisko relies on indicators, he tries to keep it simple. "Sometimes we use too many indicators and confuse ourselves," he cautions. "That is why I try not to use more than five indicators."

DON'T BUY A BREAKOUT AND OTHER RULES

"In the old days when trading was easy," Kurisko recalls, "you could buy a breakout for a few points. You'd look up stocks that were making 52-week highs on strong volume. Everyone would jump in because they knew the stock would go higher. But now, you have to watch out for a bull trap. You get a breakout, and then it reverses."

Kurisko believes that some of the reversals can be blamed on traders using high-speed computers with black-box algorithms scalping for pennies. "That's one of the reasons many traders get frustrated with the market. The timing is not like it used to be, and many of the old rules don't work like before."

One rule that Kurisko follows is using hard stops. "Stops can be the trickiest part of trading because it seems like the market takes out your stop, reverses, and goes up. Usually it's because you put your stop at the wrong place." He doesn't like to put arbitrary stops, such as a certain percentage, but lets the pattern or indicator lead him to the correct location.

When exiting a position, Kurisko likes to scale out. "I definitely like to scale in or scale out of a stock. I usually take half my shares off as Stochastics gets overbought, or it pushes against the top of the channel line. The demon in every trader is, 'What if it goes higher?' Be disciplined. Take half off because you want to catch that continuation move. If the market turns over, I'll take the rest of the position off."

Based on previous experience, Kurisko has learned how to fight greed. "There's a small little window where you're going to make money, but people always want more. They refuse to sell. Then the market drops and they want their original money back. I tell people don't think of it as a loss. Take the money and move it into another stock that is actually moving up. Instead of being stuck in a dead stock, put the money in an active stock with the same amount of cash. Force yourself to mentally exchange it."

THE DAY TRADING STIGMA

It bothers Kurisko that there are so many misconceptions about day trading. "There are many different categories of day trading," he explains. "You can be a day trader and still hold overnight. You can also trade positions intraday. I don't think it's helpful to attach a label to day traders, which seems like a stigma. You make money by taking positions when they should be taken, whether it is for a day or a couple of days. It's what works that counts."

He says that sometimes the part-time trader has an advantage. "The key is not to get chopped up intraday by the high-speed computers. Part-time traders aren't getting involved in all of the hyperactivity during the day, which is good." He adds: "Even full-time traders can learn to slow down a little and only look for trades that have the highest chance of success. Try to be more patient."

HOW TO SUCCEED AS A DAY TRADER

"If you don't have the knowledge and discipline," Kurisko cautions, "you're going to make the same mistakes that everyone else makes. You don't want to be in a position where you have to make money every day. That's why a lot of people lose money. There are times when the market is going sideways or down. It can get really rough. If you're trying to go long in a choppy market, it's hard. You don't want to be in a position where you have to make something happen. If you are looking for trades because you are bored or greedy, you'll lose money."

Once you feel comfortable and confident as a trader, he says, you almost reach a Zen-like feeling where you feel like you are one with the market. It's not like that every day, he says, but there are times when everything is going right. "You have to know where your spot is in the market."

Peter Reznicek, Professional Trader

If you want to be a successful day trader, you need a set strategy and strong discipline, says Peter Reznicek, chief strategist and cofounder of ShadowTrader.net, an advisory firm that provides intraday and position trading commentary and coaching to its clients. His main focus and expertise is in technical analysis of market internals, sector strength analysis, and identifying high-probability, low-risk, intraday and swing opportunities, in both the equity and options markets. Peter is also a principal and head trader of Translucent Capital Management, an asset management firm based in Philadelphia, PA.

HOW TO ENTER THE MARKET

"In the intraday game, it's so easy to get distracted by hundreds of different ideas," he says. "Maybe you plan on buying Apple in the morning but, if you don't have discipline, you could be punching up fifteen other stock symbols that you heard on the news. Before you know it, you're in a series of trades you didn't plan on."

Like many traders, Reznicek lets the market determine what kind of trade he'll make. "One of the most common pitfalls is people coming into the market falsely assuming they have to make money every single day," he says. "Instead, it's more a monthly or quarterly game."

The key, he explains, is to identify opportunities when they appear and not be pressured into making a trade. "Sometimes good trades jump out at you when you weren't even looking for them. Suddenly, you see a high-probability setup. The market is coming together and all of the planets are lining up."

It's important, he cautions, that you don't tell a stock how it should perform. "Why does Apple have to run up at least a dollar when it breaks out? Why does a stock that is strong in the morning going to stay strong so you can sell it at 3:59 P.M.? It doesn't make sense to impose your will on the market."

One solution, he says, is to "look at a chart and figure out where the open space in the chart is going to end. You want to trade in between areas where there is no congestion, and the next area of congestion is where the prices will be pulled like a magnet."

He explains that prices move along a path of least resistance, "The path of least resistance is where prices didn't run into congestion in the past," he says. "There are open spaces on the chart where prices can run. And those areas where prices get congested, or resisted in some manner, will be the place where prices will stop." Your price targets, he explains, are areas of support and resistance.

Nevertheless, he cautions, "You have to respect risk when day trading because things happen a lot faster and the pace is a lot quicker. With a swing trade, you often have a stop that is several dollars away. But with a day trade, your stop is a lot closer, and you can stop out in a flash. You have to be cognizant of the different pace."

DAY TRADING STRATEGIES

One of the day trading strategies that Reznicek uses is first looking for stocks he would be willing to hold long term, "but instead of holding it, I get out before the day is over," he says. "The longer time frames are really the driver of what sets up those intraday moves. It puts the odds in your favor."

Because he keeps his day trades and long-term trades separate, even if the stock continues to go up, he'll sell 75 to 90 percent of the stock before the end of the day. "If the stock closes at the high of the day, I might hold a few hundred shares overnight. Obviously, I consider this on a case-by-case basis."

But the one mistake he never makes is holding a losing stock overnight. "You have to remain flexible, but never make the trading sin of turning a day trade into a swing trade because it's a loser," Reznicek says. "It's okay to hold a few shares of a winner, but it's unacceptable to hold a loser because you think it will recover."

Another day trading strategy that Reznicek uses is an oldie but goodie: *fading the gap*. It works like this: overnight or before the market opens, the market has gapped down. And then, at the market open, the market continues to fall further.

"It's relatively rare for stocks to gap down at the open and continue lower," Reznicek says. "What usually happens is the opposite. Stocks gap down and rally up, but most gaps fill. You want to fade that gap, that is, be a buyer on the gap down, and a seller on the gap up. As a day trader, you don't want to go in the direction of the gap."

Reznicek cautions novice traders to be careful trading gaps as it takes a bit of experience to get it right. Nevertheless, doing the opposite of the crowd is often rewarding.

TECHNICAL INDICATORS

Reznicek primarily uses technical indicators to measure the breadth of the market, or the market internals. He has a few favorites. "I like the Advance-Decline Line because it tells me at any given moment how many stocks on the NYSE are advancing versus how many are declining for the day," he says. "I also use the NYSE or Nasdaq TICK, which tells me how many stocks on the entire exchange are upticking versus downticking. I think the TICK is useful as a short-term indicator."

He also looks for divergences in the TICK. For example, if the S&P 500 moved lower but the TICK didn't make an aggressive new low, it could mean the market has hit a low and might reverse.

"The market internals tell me the health of the market under the hood," he says. "Since most individual stocks follow the overall market, it makes sense to first determine the health of the overall market, and then choose individual stocks. If the market is healthy, I'm a buyer, and if the market is unhealthy and negative, I'm a seller."

Another tool that Reznicek likes is Time and Sales. "Time and Sales helps you to confirm emotions, especially if there is a speed up in the tape and you see thousands of prints going off as your stock is making a breakout." He says that unlike Level II, which is sometimes manipulated, Time and Sales tells you the trades that are actually going off.

CANDLESTICK PATTERNS

In addition to technical indicators, Reznicek looks at candlestick patterns. "I have found that most patterns can be categorized into pretty or ugly. The pretty patterns are in every book, where the stock broke out to a higher high and pulls back gently on lower volume, making a doji or hammer. In the book there's a circle around the reversal bar, and a note: 'Buy Here.' Over time you realize things don't always work out that way. What really works is the ugly pattern."

The ugly pattern, he explains, tends to fool everyone. For example, "the stock might be basing at the low of the day with a bearish flag pattern," he says, an inverted flag pattern common in downtrending stocks. "Then the stock breaks down at the bearish flag, but only by 10 or 20 cents. That's an ugly pattern. It's a failed breakdown. Everyone was looking for the pretty pattern but the stock breaks down by only a little and turns around. The odds are really strong the stock will rally hard from there."

After years of looking at patterns, Reznicek learned that often it's best to do the opposite of what the pattern says. "Why not look for a failed pattern and play it in the opposite direction?" he asks. "Do the opposite of what is not working."

Even more important than individual stock patterns, Reznicek reiterates, is looking at the direction of the broader market. "Many people make the mistake of flipping through individual stock patterns but not paying attention to the broader market. They find what they think is the right pattern, either bullish or bearish, and it fails because the market went against them."

That's another reason why Reznicek primarily uses indicators and chart patterns to look at the broader market, and not individual stocks. "You want to work top down, not bottom up."

FINAL ADVICE

If you want to day trade, Reznicek suggests that you start by paper trading and keeping a journal of what you learned. "If you are going to paper trade, use the same amount of money you'll be trading with," he suggests. "Don't simulate with a million dollars when you're only starting with $25,000. Keep detailed records and treat it like the real thing."

Shorting Strategies for Day Traders

Daytrader Timothy Sykes, author of *An American Hedge Fund* and blogger at *www.timothysykes.com*, makes more money day trading on the short side than on the long side. "My average hold time is one to two days, so I'm mainly day trading," he says. "With short selling, the quicker the better. It's sometimes scary to be the enemy of everyone on Wall Street."

Sykes compares learning about short selling to playing tennis. "When I played tennis, I hated my backhand. All I wanted to do was my forehand. But if I only worked on one stroke, I'd have a major weakness. Short selling is no different than using a forehand or backhand."

Although Sykes admits that novice traders have to be extra careful when shorting, he thinks they should learn it. "Even if you don't become a short seller, it will help you learn more lessons about the long side. You will be able to see what the other side is thinking. In the end, knowing about short selling will make you a better trader."

The stocks Sykes especially likes to short are fraudulent companies. "Let's say someone comes out with an investigative report saying a company is a fraud. Usually, these stocks will drop 10, 20, or 30 percent in a day. Even if you are a beginning trader, you want to get in when the day's low is taken out." For example, if stock XYZ dropped from $50 to $30, the minute it drops below $30, a new day's low, Sykes will sell that stock short. "A negative catalyst like a fraud accusation combined with a technical break is enough to make it a high-probability short," he says. In fact, this is his most profitable shorting strategy.

"When the stock starts cracking," Sykes notes, "people put their stop-losses right at the bottom. I call it riding a wave. You're surfing a tsunami of stop-losses. You have so many automatic computer generated stop losses, the stock may go to $29.50 in minutes. But once it cracks, the stock is gone."

Sykes cautions, however, that you have to be aware of lag times. "I'm not saying that if a stock drops 50 percent, you short it for no reason," he says. "But if it takes out a new low, especially after dip buyers have bought in, you're breaking the back of dip buyers, and fear takes over. It might tank 80 percent."

The risk, Sykes explains, is that the stock doesn't crack. "Then you've shorted right at the bottom, which is a danger. To protect myself, if a stock doesn't crack after a few minutes, I'm out. It might crack later, but because I'm trading volatile stocks, I don't want to risk a bounce."

The pattern Sykes likes is what he calls a "supernova," but what others call a parabolic move, when a stock goes vertical after the end of an extreme uptrend. "I love shorting stocks that make a parabolic move because it's mentioned on CNBC or in three newsletters," he says. "One of the strongest indicators to me is shorting on the first down day on a stock that has been up several days or weeks in a row on nothing but fluff. On that first down day, all the momentum is taken out, which leads to a morning panic, where all the stop-losses are taken out. All the momentum traders are fleeing." The key, he explains, is shorting the night before.

Another strategy Sykes likes is to short into strength, especially penny stocks under $3 a share that move on meaningless news, what he calls "pump and dumps." Companies that are under $3, he says, are his playground.

To find these stocks, he looks for volatile stocks that may be the biggest percent gainers for the day. He will also study spam e-mails touting certain stocks. "I collect those e-mails and bet against them. They are frauds and eventually get investigated."

The biggest mistake that people make, Sykes says, is shorting too early. "If a trashy stock goes from $0.25 to $1.00, it could still go to $1.75, $2.75, or $3.75. So timing is always a problem. Again, that is why I wait for the first down day that cracks the day's low. It works like a charm on momentum stocks."

Before shorting a specific stock, always make sure your brokerage firm has enough shares to borrow. Brokerage firms borrow the shares from clients who have bought the stock, and if not enough investors are long, there won't be shares.

Interestingly, Sykes doesn't short indexes like the S&P 500. "You have no advantage shorting indexes," he says. He likes to take advantage of fear, hype, and manipulation, and it is difficult to do with indexes. Syke's other top rules for shorting:

1. Don't short a rising stock just because you think it will break down.
2. If a stock you're shorting goes against you, get out. Don't give it a chance to give you a big loss.
3. Short selling is very quick, so take whatever profits the market gives you.
4. If you want to learn how to sell short, learn over time.

Chapter 8:
Doing Your Homework

The many cautionary comments included in this book are not designed to discourage you, but to alert you to the challenges you face. After all, it's estimated that no more than 5 percent of people who try make a consistently profitable living as a day trader. If you're determined to be a day trader, you won't be deterred by what anyone says or writes. I know of day traders who struggled for years before they finally made it. They really loved to day trade. They also loved the fact they could achieve something that most people only dream about.

On the other hand, after reading this book, if you now believe that day trading isn't for you, I'm delighted if I helped you with your decision. In the end, you saved time and money. Also, if day trading is something you're doing because you think it's an easy way to make money, then I will have saved you a fortune: It's not an easy way to make money. If you don't take the time to learn the skills or have the discipline to follow the rules, then you shouldn't day trade. Just like not everyone can be a professional golfer or a doctor, not everyone is suited to be a day trader.

Before you can day trade, you really must understand yourself and your personality. That is one reason why so many rookies lose money that first year. The emotional challenges of being a day trader are ten times more difficult than learning the tools and software.

The Patient Day Trader

Hopefully, you also learned that you don't need to make hundreds of trades a day to be successful. Sometimes the smartest move you can make is to stay on the sidelines. Although he is not a day trader, here is what best-selling author and investor Jim Rogers said in the book, Market Wizards: "One of the best rules anybody can learn about investing is to do nothing, absolutely nothing, until there is something to do. . . . I just wait until there is money lying in the corner, and all I have to do is go over there and pick it up. I do nothing in the meantime."

Rogers waits until he finds investments that have a high probability of success and, if he can't find any, he patiently waits for the next opportunity.

What You Can Learn from Day Traders

Although many people tease day traders for having such a short-term mindset, they can teach you a lot of lessons. For example, day traders learn early that to survive they must get out of losing stocks quickly. It's rare to hear a professional day trader say, "I hope . . ." when monitoring a stock. They don't rely on hope, but on tools and charts, as well as discipline, guts, and the ability to make fast decisions under stress. These are just a few of the habits of highly successful day traders.

See the Bigger Picture

Even though you're a day trader, it's always useful to keep your eye on the bigger picture, either when using charts or analyzing market trends. Sometimes people get so focused on the small details they don't recognize what's really going on. It's a lot easier to be bullish in a bull market and bearish in a bear market, as legendary trader Jesse Livermore once said.

And finally, try to keep it simple. The flashing lights and bright colors distract too many traders, but to really succeed you want to focus on what is really important. It takes time, but eventually you will learn how.

Become a Student of the Market

Even after reading this book, you may still have a lot of questions. One question new traders often ask is: "How long will it take to become profitable?" Instead, you should ask, "How much effort is required before I really know what I'm doing?" Although the answer is different for each person, doing your homework is the key.

Before you place your first trade, read books, study, and explore before committing real money to the market. Understanding the stock market is a continuous, lifelong pursuit. Although this book provides you a useful introduction to day trading, the next step is yours. Below are some additional resources, including other books, which will help you on your journey.

As mentioned earlier, if you have any questions while reading this book, call the Help Desk at your local brokerage firm. As long as you're a customer, the representatives at your brokerage firm should answer your questions.

Getting Stock Ideas

You may be ready to get started but wonder how to get stock ideas. That's a very good question! First, many experienced traders rely on real-time stock scanners to provide them with day trading candidates. This could be third-party software or stocks included in your brokerage firm's trading platform. The goal is to find stocks that are volatile enough to make you money, but not necessarily the most volatile. Also, many traders create a watch list of stocks that may be good candidates for day trading (many of these stocks appear on the most active stock lists). Over time, you will add dozens (or only a few) stocks to your watch list. Soon you'll have a universe of stocks, and stock sectors, that you'll observe on a daily basis.

If you want additional stock ideas, you can listen to and watch a professional day trader in action. Visit *www.daytradingradio.com* for a live, continuous feed of day trader John Kurisko, who I interviewed for this book. You can watch him make trades, explain how to use technical indicators, identify patterns, pick out stocks to buy or sell, and interview guests. This will give you a real-life look into one day trader's world, and also help expand on what you've learned in this book. Finally, if you're wondering how to choose your first stock, watching Kurisko will give you some ideas. (For your information, I am not affiliated with Day Trading Radio in any way).

A Day in the Life of a Day Trader

For additional insights, the following diary can give you clues of how other traders prepare for the upcoming market day. Keep in mind that every day trader has a personalized trading plan, so there is no one right way. Also, because portions of this diary are from experienced traders, don't worry if some of the ideas seem confusing.

7:00 P.M. (ET). The night before market opening:

- Review both profitable and unprofitable trades and enter notes into your trading diary.
- Write the lessons learned, and review any previous mistakes. You will make mistakes, but the goal is not allowing yourself to repeat them.
- If any positions were held overnight, be certain that the reason for holding is still valid. Constantly re-evaluate current trades.
- Start planning a strategy for the following day.

9:30 P.M. (ET)

- Scan individual charts for buying or selling ideas.
- Put a handful of technical indicators on a chart for clues to market direction.
- Begin formulating a trading plan.

8:00 A.M. (ET)

- Scan financial newspapers and financial websites such as Marketwatch, Briefing, Yahoo! Finance, and Bloomberg for breaking news and potential stock ideas.
- Arrange stock charts, order entry screens, and technical indicators.
- Turn on financial television programs like CNBC or Bloomberg.
- Observe the major market indexes such as the Dow Jones Industrial Average (DJIA), the S&P 500, and the Nasdaq Composite for clues as to market direction.
- Observe stock sectors for strength or weakness.
- Decide what indexes or individual stocks to trade based on previous research.
- Review a list of stocks or exchange-traded funds (ETFs).

Many traders write down the specific steps they need to take in a "trading checklist," similar to what a pilot might use before takeoff. Also, be sure to get plenty of rest, food, and exercise before trading. You must have a clear head before the market opens. And if you feel out of synch with the market, that's okay. Take the day off, or at least get away from the computer and return when you're ready for your "A" game.

9:30 A.M.(ET). At the market open:

- Manage all current positions. Take advantage of breakouts to get out of any bad trades in your portfolio. If you have any doubts, exit the trade.
- Continue monitoring stock or ETF sectors. Identify individual stocks or ETFs to trade.
- Study market indicators to monitor the market, and look at technical indicators for clues as to market direction. Indicators may help you determine entry and exit points.

3:30 P.M. (ET). Market closes in thirty minutes:

- Day traders close out any open positions

4:00 P.M. (ET). Market closes.

FIG 8.1: The Day Trader   Artist: Randy Ruether

The Closing Bell:
Going Forward

Now that you have a better idea what it means to be a day trader, it's your decision what to do next. You may continue learning and researching and take my advice to practice trade before committing real money into the market. Or you may open up your first trading account. Either way, one of my goals was to prepare you emotionally for a tough battle.

As you go forward, remember to keep educating yourself. There will always be something new to learn: new technology, new strategies, and new software. As the market changes over time, and as new rules are added or removed, there will always be opportunities for those who are informed and alert to make money.

I want to thank you for taking the time to read my book. If I've been able to help you make or save money, I'd be very pleased. Most important to me, I hope I've motivated you to keep learning about the stock market.

Good luck, and be sure to take it one day at a time.

How to Contact Me

Feel free to write me at *msincere@gmail.com* if you have any questions, or visit my website at *www.michaelsincere.com*. Also, if you notice any errors, which are my responsibility, please let me know.

As always, I'm delighted to hear from you.

Appendix A:
Resources for Day Traders

Books for Novice Day Traders

Technical Analysis Plain and Simple (FT Press, 3rd Edition, 2010) by Michael Kahn

An easy-to-read introduction to technical analysis and technical indicators.

The Complete Idiots Guide to Technical Analysis (Alpha, 2010) by Jan Arps

An introductory book about technical analysis written in a user-friendly tone.

How to Make Money in Stocks (McGraw-Hill, 4th Edition, 2009) by William J. O'Neil

This bestseller shows investors how to profit in the market by using a rule-based, systematic approach.

The Visual Investor: How to Spot Market Trends (Wiley, 2009) by John J. Murphy

A thoughtful introduction to technical analysis and the nuances of using technical indicators.

The Truth about Day Trading Stocks (Wiley, 2009) by Josh DiPietro

A first-person account about the trials and tribulations of being a day trader, and what the author learned along the way.

How I Made $200,000,000 in the Stock Market (Martino Fine Books, Revised, 2009) by Nicolas Darvas

Old bestseller of how a stock market newbie makes a fortune in the stock market using support and resistance.

A Beginner's Guide to Short-Term Trading (Adams Media, 2008) by Toni Turner

An easy-to-read bestseller aimed at novice traders about short-term trading tactics and tools, including technical indicators.

A Beginner's Guide to Day Trading Online (Adams Media, 2007) by Toni Turner

This groundbreaking bestseller was the first to give a step-by-step explanation of day trading for beginners with a friendly, humorous voice.

Day Trading for Dummies (Wiley, 2007) by Ann Logue

A general overview of day trading written in a friendly voice.

Market Wizards (Marketplace Books, Classic Edition, 2006) and *New Market Wizards* (Marketplace Books, 2008), by Jack Schwager

The author delves into the minds of profitable traders in these two classics.

Reminiscences of a Stock Operator (Wiley, Revised, 2006) by Edwin Lefevre

Must-read classic about the trading experiences of Jesse Livermore, a legendary trader from the early twentieth century.

Technical Analysis for Dummies (Wiley, 2004) by Barbara Rockefeller

An introductory book about technical analysis written in a user-friendly tone.

High Probability Trading (McGraw-Hill, 2003) by Marcel Link
Entertaining and realistic book about how to succeed as a high-probability trader.

Trading for a Living (Wiley, 1993) by Alexander Elder
Bestselling book on how to master the psychological challenges of the market as well as how to use technical indicators when trading.

The Disciplined Trader (Prentice-Hall, 1990) by Mark Douglas
Bestseller on the psychology of trading and what it takes to overcome your own emotions.

Books for Experienced Traders

Super Trader (McGraw-Hill, 2009) by Van K. Tharp
The Ultimate Day Trader (Adams Media, 2009) by Jake Bernstein
Candlestick Charting Explained (McGraw-Hill, 2006), by Gregory Morris
Come Into My Trading Room (Wiley, 2002) by Alexander Elder
Technical Analysis Explained (McGraw-Hill, 2002) by Martin J. Pring
Trading in the Zone (Prentice Hall, 2001) by Mark Douglas
Japanese Candlestick Charting Techniques (Prentice Hall, 2001) by Steve Nison
Technical Analysis from A to Z (McGraw-Hill, 2000) by Steven B. Achelis
Technical Analysis of the Financial Markets (NY Institute of Finance, 1999) by John J. Murphy

Useful Websites for Traders and Investors

finance.yahoo.com (Yahoo! Finance)

money.cnn.com (Money)

www.activetrademag.com (Active Trader Magazine)

www.barrons.com (Barrons)

www.bigcharts.com (Big Charts)

www.bloomberg.com (Bloomberg)

www.briefing.com (Briefing)

www.candlecharts.com (Candlecharts)

www.cboe.com (Chicago Board Options Exchange)

www.cnbc.com (CNBC)

www.decisionpoint.com (Decision Point)

www.daytradingradio.com (Day Trading Radio)

www.fool.com (Motley Fool)

www.forbes.com (Forbes Magazine)

www.ft.com (Financial Times)

www.google.com/finance (Google Finance)

www.investopedia.com (Investopedia)

www.investors.com (Investor's Business Daily)

www.investorwords.com (Investor Words)

www.ise.com (International Securities Exchange)

www.kiplinger.com (Kiplingers)

www.marketwatch.com (Marketwatch)

www.moneyshow.com (The Money Show)

www.morningstar.com (Morningstar)

www.nasdaq.com (Nasdaq)

www.nyse.com (New York Stock Exchange)

www.optionseducation.org (Options Industry Council)

www.quote.com (Quote.com)

www.seekingalpha.com (Seeking Alpha)

www.sfomag.com (Stocks, Futures, and Options magazine)

www.smartmoney.com (Smart Money)

www.stockcharts.com (Stockcharts)

www.thekirkreport.com (The Kirk Report)

www.thestreet.com (Real Money and The Street)

www.traders.com (Stock and Commodities magazine)

www.tradersexpo.com (Trader's Expo)

www.tradersnarrative.com (Trader's Narrative)

www.tradingmarkets.com (Trading Markets)

www.wsj.com (Wall Street Journal)

Stock Discussion Groups

The following are a few of the more popular trading groups. Use an Internet search engine to find more:

groups.google.com (Google)

messages.yahoo.com (Yahoo!)

www.elitetrader.com (Elite Trader)

www.investors.com (IBD Community)

www.investorvillage.com (Investor Village)

www.ragingbull.com (Raging Bull)

www.siliconinvestor.com (Silicon Investor)

www.trade2win.com (Trade 2 Win)

www.traders-talk.com (Trader's Talk)

Appendix B:
Glossary of Terms

Advance-Decline Line

This indicator plots a running total of advancing stocks minus the declining stocks each day.

After-hours market

After the regular market closes, the after-hours market allows investors and traders to buy and sell individual securities. This market is open from 4:00 P.M. to 8:00 P.M. (ET).

All or none (AON)

An instruction given to a brokerage firm that requires that the shares in an order are filled completely or not at all.

Arms Index (TRIN)

This breadth indicator helps identify overbought and oversold conditions.

Ascending triangle

Bullish pattern that forms during an uptrend and resembles a triangle

Ask price (or offer)

The lowest price a seller is willing to accept for an individual security; the price that is offered for sale.

Bear market

A stock market environment where investors are gloomy, the prices of stocks and other securities are falling, and the broad market indexes have plunged by 20 percent or more off of its highs.

Bid price

It's the highest price a buyer is willing to pay for an individual security. Also the best price the seller will receive for a security sold at the market price.

Bollinger Bands

This indicator helps traders to identify overbought and oversold conditions.

Bond

A type of loan issued by government, local municipality, or company in order to raise capital.

Breakout

Price movement that rises above or below support or resistance on heavy volume.

Buy-and-hold

Investment strategy in which an investor buys stocks and holds indefinitely, regardless of short-term fluctuations in the market.

Buying power

The total cash held in a brokerage account that is available for traders to buy securities (plus the ability to borrow and use existing priorities as collateral).

Buy-stop order

An order to buy a security that is above the current ask price.

Call option

A call option is a financial contract that gives buyers the right, but not the obligation, to buy an asset by a certain date if certain obligations are met.

Candlestick

Popular type of price chart that displays the high, low, open, and close of each time period and can be used to give trading signals.

Capital gain

A profit, or gain, that is realized when an asset, such as a stock, bond, or real estate, is sold for a price higher than the original purchase price.

Capital loss

A loss that is realized when an asset is sold for a price lower than the original purchase price.

Dark cloud cover

In candlestick charts, a bearish price pattern where a black candlestick follows a long white candlestick.

Divergence

When the price of an asset moves in the opposite direction of an indicator.

Dragonfly doji

In candlestick charts, a price pattern that reflects indecision on behalf of traders. The stock's opening and closing price are equal and indicates the trend may be at a turning point.

Drawdown

The amount of equity your account lost as a result of a trade or a series of trades.

Exchange-traded funds (ETF)

An investment fund that trades like a stock but tracks an index, commodity, currency, or basket of assets like stocks.

Exponential moving average

A type of moving average used to anticipate long-term trends. It shows the average value of the underlying data, where more weight is given to the most recent time periods.

Federal Reserve (the Fed)
Created in 1913, the Fed is the central banking system of the United States, responsible for overseeing money supply, interest rates, and credit.

Fill or kill
An instruction to the brokerage to either fill the trader's order entirely or cancel it.

Flash crash
This is the May 6, 2010, stock market crash that caused the stock market to plunge over 600 points within minutes, before recovering the losses. It was blamed on an errant E-mini option futures order.

Fundamental analysis
This is a method of evaluating a stock or other security by examining the underlying business, such as financial statements, competitors, and management.

Futures contract
This is a contract between two parties to buy or sell an asset (e.g., commodities, currencies, options) on a specified future date for a specified price.

Good 'Til Canceled (GTC)

This is an instruction to your brokerage firm to keep an order to buy or sell a security active until the limit price has been reached, even if it takes days or weeks.

Hammer

The hammer is a candlestick pattern that forms when a security moves much lower after the open, but rallies to close above the intraday low.

Hedge

A hedge is used to limit losses and involves taking a position in one security that offsets a position in a related security.

High-frequency trading

This is a computerized trading strategy that uses powerful computers and complex algorithms to make many trades at fast speeds with short holding periods.

Intraday

This term means you are buying or selling securities within a single trading day.

Lagging indicator

This is a technical indicator that follows, or lags, the price of an underlying security.

Level I quote
Level I quotes are the most current real-time bid and ask quotes for any stock.

Level II quote
Level II quotes are the most current real-time bid and ask quotes for Nasdaq market makers.

Level III
Level III is a trading service that allows NASD member firms to enter quotes and execute orders.

Leverage
Leverage is a technique where borrowed capital is used to multiply gains or losses, and can increase (or decrease) the investment return.

Liquidity
Liquidity refers to how quickly you can get into or out of a security at the same price level.

Long position
A long position means the investor is holding a security, hoping to profit if the price goes up.

Margin account

A margin account refers to a type of a brokerage account where a customer can borrow cash from the brokerage firm to buy securities.

Margin call

This is a call from a brokerage firm to a customer that demands he or she pay enough cash to satisfy the maintenance requirements (and the Federal Reserve Board rule, Regulation T) to cover against an unfavorable price movement.

Market indicator

A market indicator, which can be technical, sentiment, fundamental, or economic, generates signals that give clues and insight into future market direction.

Market maker

A member of an exchange (usually refers to Nasdaq) that makes a market for a particular security and ensures there is enough liquidity for that security.

Market order

This is an order to buy or sell a stock at the current market price.

Mental stop

This is a stop-loss but is not actually entered as an order; but is written on paper or remembered.

Option

An option is a contract that gives you the right, but not the obligation, to buy or sell an underlying security at a specific price for a specific time period.

Oscillator

A term used in technical analysis that refers to a type of indicator that moves up and down, or oscillates, within a price range.

Overbought

Overbought refers to a condition when demand for a security is so strong that the price has risen too high.

Oversold

Oversold refers to a condition when demand for a security is so weak that the price has dropped too low.

Pattern day trader

An SEC designation for those who buy and sell a security at least four times within a five-day period and are now subject to certain rules, such as maintaining at least $25,000 in a brokerage account.

Position trading

Position trading is a trading strategy where securities are held from several days to months.

Put

A put is a financial contract that gives buyers the right, but not the obligation, to sell an asset by a certain date if certain obligations are met.

Resistance

On a stock chart, this a price level where sellers prevent a stock from rising higher.

Retracement

On a stock chart, retracement means that the price of a security temporarily changes direction; in other words, it's a temporary price reversal.

Reversal

On a stock chart, reversal means that the price of a security changes direction.

Rising window

A candlestick pattern when yesterday's high is below today's low, leaving a gap, or hole, in the daily price chart.

Risk-reward ratio

A ratio used by investors and traders when the risk of a particular trade is weighed against the potential return.

Scale in or out

Scaling in and out means you get into or out of a position in increments as the price rises or falls.

Scalping

This is a day trading strategy where you make profits on small price movements.

Securities and Exchange Commission (SEC)

The SEC is a government commission created by Congress and appointed by the U.S. president to regulate the securities markets and protect investors from fraud and manipulation.

Security

An investment instrument such as a stock, bond, certificate of interest, or option, to name just a few.

Share

A unit of ownership issued to shareholders by a corporation.

Shooting star

This is a candlestick chart pattern that is formed during an uptrend and may signal a reversal.

Shorting (sell short)

This is the practice of borrowing shares of stock from a brokerage firm and buying them back later at a lower price, hopefully for a profit.

Slippage

When using a market order, the difference between the estimated price and the actual execution price.

Specialist

A member of an exchange (usually refers to the New York Stock Exchange) that makes a market for a particular security and ensures there is enough liquidity for that security.

Spread

The difference between the bid and ask price of a security.

Stochastics

Stochastics is an indicator that helps determine whether a security is overbought or oversold.

Support

On a stock chart, this a price level where buyers prevent a stock from falling further.

Swing trading

A trading strategy that seeks to create profits by holding positions for relatively short periods, often from two to five days.

Technical analysis

A method of evaluating securities and attempting to anticipate future stock prices based on price and volume.

Technical indicator

An indicator displayed on a chart that attempts to anticipate future price movements of a security.

Tick

This refers to the upward or downward movement in the price of a security.

Ticker symbol

These are the letters used to identify a security listed on the exchanges.

Time and Sales

Time and Sales displays information about the most current trade of a security, including time, price, and lot size.

Trading range
Trading range refers to a security trading between high and low prices on a chart.

Trailing stop
This is an automated order, set as a percentage or by points, that adjusts upward or downward as your stock advances, or falls, in price.

Trend
Trend refers to the current direction or movement of a security. Downtrend is when overall direction is down, and uptrend is when overall direction is up.

Trendline
A straight line that connects at least two price pivot points, either two pivot lows in an uptrend, or two pivot highs in a downtrend.

Triangle
This is a chart pattern that resembles a triangle in which the price gets narrower over time because of lower tops and higher bottoms.

Volatility
Volatility refers to the rate at which a security moves up and down over a period of time.

Volume

Volume refers to the number of shares of a security traded during a certain time period.

Wedge

A chart resembling a triangle, where the price gets narrower over time, but both lines have the same trend but different slopes.

Acknowledgments

To Peter Archer, acquisitions editor at Adams Media, for giving me the opportunity to write this book and for patiently working with me until it was completed; and to content editor Jennifer Lawler for doing a superb job.

I am also grateful to Siranirin Rattananiphon for always being there for me.

Also, to Harvey Small, Jason Zimmer, Karina Benzineb, Karolina Roubickovi, Hazel Diana Garcia, and Anna Ridolfo for listening; Toni Turner for her encouragement and ideas, and for always giving me great quotes; Paula Florez, my extremely helpful assistant; Alexandra Bengtsson, who has always been fascinated by day trading; cartoonist Randy Ruether, photographer Sean Murdock, and web designer Ryan Saunders; Adam Banker for his help behind the scenes; Matt Heien for his promotional efforts.

Also, without the help of the following experts, this book could not have been written: traders John Kurisko, Peter Reznicek, Timothy Sykes, and Toni Turner; Marcel Link for sharing his insights about the emotional demands of trading; Charles Kirk for letting me know the pros and cons of being a trader; Simon Maierhofer for his knowledge about ETFs; Joe Harwood for sharing his detailed knowledge about options; Tom McClellan for his help with the McClellan Oscillator; Steve Nison for his insights into trading with candlesticks, and Mark Wolfinger for making very detailed suggestions.

Index

About the Author

Michael Sincere is the author of a number of investment and trading books, including *Understanding Stocks* (McGraw-Hill, 2003), the bestselling *Understanding Options* (McGraw-Hill, 2006), and *All About Market Indicators* (McGraw-Hill, 2010), to name just a few.

As a financial journalist, Sincere has written hundreds of columns and magazine articles on investing and trading, including a monthly column for MarketWatch on market indicators. He has been interviewed on dozens of national radio programs and has appeared on several financial news programs, including CNBC and ABC's *World News Now!* to talk about his books.

Sincere also finished his first novel, *The Last Au Pair*, about the exciting adventures of a group of European au pairs living in South Florida. The book will be prereleased on Kindle, Nook, and Apple in January 2011.